The Elements
of Academic Success

Other books by Gene Kizer, Jr.

ISBN: 978-0-9853632-0-8 (eBook)

Charleston Athenaeum Press

The Elements of Academic Success

How to Graduate Magna Cum Laude from College

(or how to just graduate, PERIOD!)

Gene Kizer, Jr.

CHARLESTON ATHENAEUM PRESS

Charleston Athenaeum Press
www.CharlestonAthenaeumPress.com

Post Office Box 13012
Charleston, South Carolina 29422-3012

*(Please visit our website and join our
New Publication Notification List)*

ISBN: 978-0-9853632-1-5 *(softcover)*
ISBN: 978-0-9853632-9-1 *(eBook)*

First Print Edition
January, 2014

To Dad

No man ever had a better Dad.

From the beginning, he has believed in this book and encouraged me to write it. And now it is here – to help students make good grades, achieve their goals, enrich their lives, and contribute to the good of mankind for years to come.

To Mom,
Rest in peace

She always emphasized education and every day before school joked and said "Make a hundred!"... **but she wasn't joking!**

To My Children, Trey and Travis, and to Trey's Heather

So proud of my boys, and Heather! They are grown, on their own, working hard and doing great.

> *... and we all embrace the values of Lt. Richard Sharpe, Commander of the 'Chosen Men,' the Sharpshooters of the 2nd Battalion in His Britannic Majesty's 95th Rifle Corps, and of Sergeant Patrick Harper.*

To My Stepmother, Elaine Bonner

Dad found romance on the golf course and met his lovely June bride there, which is fitting because the first golf played in America was played here in romantic Charleston!

To Clay and Kim Martin

Friends so close that I spent the first night of their honeymoon with them! *(I was on the couch, of course!)*. That was four decades ago. People don't come any better than this.

In Memoriam

Clark G. Reynolds
Professor of History

December 11, 1939 - December 10, 2005

Good friend. Beloved and accomplished professor. He loved the nighttime sky. He regularly stepped outside of his house in the wee hours to marvel at the stars and constellations. His *Cosmos in History* course at the College of Charleston taught me more about human beings and human nature (it never changes – it has been the same forever and will remain the same, forever) than any other course I took or book I read.

He was an author many times over and a nationally recognized naval historian who loved his country and believed in its goodness.

He had a tremendous, almost imposing presence in the classroom, yet was so encouraging and approachable. He tolerated no disrespect such as wearing hats or chewing gum. In his classroom, students came to learn. His fascinating, comprehensive trademark – his chronological time-lines of the people and events of history being discussed that day – filled up every chalk board before every class and sometimes went halfway around the room. They greatly enhanced his lectures.

He knew how to teach and used every tool possible such as video, music, art, his own authoritative voice speaking German time to time, his expertise in military history since so much of human history is about war.

He was from the old school. He imparted knowledge easily and confidently. He stimulated his students because he was stimulated himself. He was interested in so much and had learned so much in his life. He made his students think, think, think, about everything.

We disagreed on the causes of the War Between the States. I'm a Southerner and he was a Californian who sympathized with the North. But he encouraged me to make my argument and write exactly what I wanted to write in my bachelor's essay for History Departmental Honors, which he directed – as long as I backed it up with impeccable scholarship.[1]

I made an "A++" (he gave me two pluses on that paper!) though I know there were some historical interpretations with which he disagreed as a scholar. As I said, he was from the old school, a better school, and was not some cowardly politically correct "historian." He was a real scholar and gentleman.

And he loved jazz! One time we had to drive across town. We got in his car. He turned the key and the stereo blasted me out! I'm surprised a window didn't break! He quickly turned it down, slightly embarrassed. He had had it LOUD on his commute to the College of Charleston that morning across the Cooper River Bridge from his Mt. Pleasant home, windows up, music blaring, savoring that New Orleans sound he loved so much.

He always stood up for what was right, especially when opposed by ignorance and intolerance, and he batted a thousand.

---

[1] Gene H. Kizer, Jr., "Economic Arguments and Justifications for Southern Secession, 1850s to 1861" (Bachelor's Essay, College of Charleston, 2000), Addlestone Library Special Collections.

Contents

(with each chapter's epigraph)

In Memoriam: Professor Clark G. Reynolds   ix

Author's Note   xix

I
Start Strong
Be Organized and in Control

Page 3

By recording the dates on which you need to START assignments, you give yourself a perfect blueprint for the entire semester, especially those times when things stack up. In college, there are things going on all the time, but you will be able to coordinate everything. Your weeks will be extremely productive and satisfying by planning them around your calendar.

II
Professors

Page 39

Most professors are decent people who enjoy teaching their material and really want you to succeed in their classes, but some are unquestionably better than others, and some are unquestionably harder graders than others. You'll have to decide the best fit for you.

III
Class
Page 68

Write fast, but write down everything that comes out of a professor's mouth. That's what I did at the College of Charleston. It is invaluable to have notes like that when test time rolls around. You have a lot of options for producing homemade study guides from a good set of notes, and at the very least, you will be able to go through your notebook and highlight the most important things, tag pages, etc.

IV
Grades
Page 90

The actual quotation belongs to Confucius: "Choose a job you love, and you will never have to work a day in your life." **This is the foundation of all happiness and success.** If you do what you love, you will be so stimulated by what you do, it won't seem like work. It will be fun! So, pursue with all your heart, your dreams and goals and the things that stimulate you! Have success, achieve some great things, make money, find a partner who makes you happy and live a great life!

V
Studying Effectively
Page 105

Constantly reading, writing, working problems, researching, thinking, struggling with another language's vocabulary, and the other challenges one faces in college, unquestionably increase intellectual capacity. It's no different from training for a physical competition. One works the body hard, running, weightlifting, swimming, bike riding, and as a result, the body gets stronger, faster, healthier, and the individual is happier, more confident, and more powerful. The intellectual rigors of college life increase a student's brain power, and that increased brain power is there for everything in the student's life, from sports, to achievement of personal goals, to wooing a love interest. Brainpower is the key to happiness, and the more one has, the better.

VI
Preparing for Tests/Exams
Page 128

Exam Preparation Triage... There will be many times when you have several tests, papers or other work all due the same week, especially at mid-term. When that happens, do what military doctors and nurses do after a battle when wounded soldiers are lying around bleeding and drying: analyze the situation and save the largest number you can in the shortest period of time by going to those who can be stabilized quickly, then moving to the more needy.

VII
Taking Tests/Exams
Page 156

Most professors like to see an outline. They know the value of outlines. You can score points with a good outline, and it will help you remember everything as well as organize your writing and make it more persuasive. Be as neat with your outline as with your answer itself.

VIII
Papers and Writing
Page 165

The first lesson: DON'T GET STUCK. If you get stuck, get yourself unstuck quick, any way you can. People get stuck because they act like wimps and whine and stare at the wall and feel sorry for themselves. Don't be a big baby. Fire up your brain! Be a man or a woman! Put some words down on paper! Put some clay on the potter's wheel and get going!

The second lesson: An EXCELLENT method of writing is to write your first draft straight from your brain without stopping to look at your sources. Just write what you know and keep moving as fast as possible. The writing is so much more natural and comes easier than when you refer back, constantly, to books, articles and notes.

IX
Presentations
Page 216

"A lawyer friend of mine – a great guy, a very smart guy – came up to me the other day and said he heard that I had spoken in front of 62,000 people in Los Angeles. He said, 'How do you do that? Don't you get scared?' I said, 'I don't want to think about it.' It is true: I don't want to think about it. I just do it. Then he called me up the next day and said, 'That's the smartest thing I've ever heard.'"—Donald Trump[30]

X
Continue Strong
Winning, and the Philosophy of Success
Page 234

"Winning is not everything. It is the only thing."
– Vince Lombardi

"Whether you believe you can do a thing or believe you can't, you are right." – Henry Ford

"The longer I live, the more deeply I am convinced that that which makes the difference between one man and another – between the weak and the powerful, the great and the insignificant – is energy, invincible determination, a purpose once

formed and then death or victory."
– Fowell Buxton

"Success or failure in business is caused more by mental attitude even than by mental capacities."
– Walter Dill Scott

"You can really have everything you want. If you go after it. But you will have to want it. The desire for success must be so strong within you that it is the very breath of your life — your first thought when you awaken in the morning, your last thought when you go to bed at night."
– Charles E. Popplestone

"The starting point of all achievement is desire. Keep this constantly in mind. Weak desires bring weak results, just as a small amount of fire makes a small amount of heat." – Napoleon Hill

"People do not lack strength; they lack will."
– Victor Hugo

"Success isn't a result of spontaneous combustion. You must set yourself on fire." – Arnold H. Glasow

"It's not the size of the man in the fight, it's the size of the fight in the man." – Teddy Roosevelt

Index of All 351 Bold Topic Sections by Chapter   296
Author's Final Note   327
Colophon   330
Bibliography   333

Author's Note

I did not name this book *The Elements of Academic Success, How to Graduate **Summa** Cum Laude from College*, because I, myself, graduated **magna** cum laude, even though I came close to graduating summa cum laude.

So I opted to subtitle the book according to what I could write about with absolute authority: *How to Graduate **Magna Cum Laude** from College.*

Of course, the principles are the same for all honors: cum laude, magna cum laude, or summa cum laude. If you want to graduate summa cum laude, work even harder and more focused.

Some of this book is powerful common sense. For students, seeing common sense in writing and enhanced, validates it and strengthens it.

Students should read over the "Index of All 351 Bold Topic Sections by Chapter" in the back of the book. The numbered topic sections are *easy* to go through, and the things a student needs will jump out at them.

Students should also focus on specific chapters when they need them. For example, if a student has important papers on the horizon, they should

read "VIII, Papers and Writing" as soon as
possible.

All students should read the first chapter:
"I, Start Strong, *Be Organized and in Control*."

It would be good for a student to skim over the
entire book as soon as possible and read anything
that will help them.

Many many heartfelt thanks to everyone
who has contributed to this book in any way,
especially people who work in libraries
and my very fine professors at alma mater,
the College of Charleston, in Charleston,
South Carolina, founded in 1770.

Also, **many heartfelt thanks** to my very fine
professors at The Citadel, The Military College
of South Carolina, where I took some outstanding
graduate English courses.

The College of Charleston is dedicated to a policy
of NO grade inflation, such as that which has
plagued some well-known schools in recent years.
If you get an A at C of C, you earned it and it
means something.

I am not Albert Einstein, but I consistently made
"A"s at the College of Charleston because I was
ON FIRE to graduate magna cum laude. I was
obsessed, and I knew what I wanted to study, and
I shied away from nothing.

I developed highly effective skills and techniques that helped me make "A"s in nearly everything, and my attitude was strong, positive and tenacious.

Attitude is the only thing in life a person has total control over.

Your attitude will bring you success and happiness, or bring you misery.

Readers of this book will absorb my proven techniques and aggressive NOT-GOING-TO-BE-DENIED attitude.

That attitude will help them excel in college, and in life.

———————————

It was in the halls of the College of Charleston and the classrooms of my professors that this book was conceived.

And now it is born onto the printed page to inspire and empower students everywhere.

Gene Kizer, Jr.
Charleston, South Carolina
January, 2014

The Elements
of Academic Success

The energy of the mind is the essence of life.

—Aristotle

I
Start Strong
Be Organized and in Control

By recording the dates on which you need to START assignments, you give yourself a perfect blueprint for the entire semester, especially those times when things stack up. In college, there are things going on all the time, but you will be able to coordinate everything. Your weeks will be extremely productive and satisfying by planning them around your calendar.

1. Buy an inexpensive desk calendar.

Buy a big desk calendar for around $4 from somewhere like Staples, or get a calendar with enough space to write under each day. The moment you get the syllabi for all of your courses, go through the entire semester and put down every test, paper, presentation, field trip, final exam – everything for every course – under the appropriate date.

I can not begin to tell you how important this is. Once the semester is laid out, you will be able to see clearly those periods of time when things stack up, such as several tests in the same week, or tests at the same time that term papers, presentations or book reviews are due.

There are so many important things to put on your calendar. For some courses you might have to attend concerts or plays, or take field trips. The calendar helps you organize it all and see into the future. It is a crystal ball. Your calendar will enable you to anticipate and plan well in advance for those weeks in which multiple tests or other assignments fall.

I know this seems like common sense, and it is, but it is imperative that you think this way. Get a calendar and mark it up.

2. Go further. Put down the dates on which you need to begin each assignment.

You will already know when tests or papers are coming up because they will be on your calendar, *but here is the key to success:* Backtrack and note on your calendar the date by which you must BEGIN each assignment in order to have plenty of time to earn your "A."

Put down the exact date to begin studying so that you have four or five days to prepare for a major exam.

Put down the exact date to begin research for a paper, and the exact date to start writing.

Put down the exact date by which you need to

begin working lots of math problems for a math test. Math, sciences and foreign languages are especially critical because knowledge builds on previous knowledge as you go through the semester. If you get behind in math, science or a foreign language, you are DEAD. You just can't learn math by skimming over math problems. You have to wrestle with them and work them, the more the better. The same with foreign languages. You have to learn vocabulary, pronounce words, translate, etc.

Put on your calendar the exact date to begin working on a presentation, and the exact date to start practicing out loud in your home (e.g., practice out loud at least two or three days before you have to stand up in front of the class).

By recording the dates on which you need to start assignments, you give yourself a perfect blueprint for the entire semester, especially those times when things stack up. In college, there are things going on all the time, but you will be able to coordinate everything. Your weeks will be extremely productive and satisfying by planning them around your calendar.

Your calendar really is sort of magical and should be viewed as part of your brain. Use it to enhance your personal power and brainpower with organization.

3. Another reason to know everything that is coming up: Fear of the unknown.

Fear of the unknown is a drain. If you don't have a calendar, you will still know in the back of your mind that a deadline is approaching and it will drive you crazy. With a calendar, *nothing* sneaks up on you. *You* have total control and the ability to deal with everything. Plan each week around your calendar and you will never be overwhelmed.

You'll also be able to utilize your breaks with greater effectiveness. If you are behind in something and fall break is coming up, instead of going out of town for five days, go out for three and use the other two to catch up or get ahead. You have to think this way because it will enable you to have a life yet still do good in school.

4. If you don't take control of your coursework and schedule, you are blowing in the wind.

You are courting frustration. You will be a weak student.

It is powerful to have a good calendar and know where you are going every single week during the semester. It is good to do this in life.

It is weak to drift, causes frustration, and usually wastes time. Wasting time is wasting your life. Life is too short to waste any of it.

Having a good calendar and being organized

will also help you party more. You will anticipate your assignments and often get them done early. Then you can head out the door feeling good.

5. Make SURE you understand how much everything counts toward your grade.

Keep front and center the percentage that tests, papers and exams will count. Write it inside the front cover of a notebook and on your calendar.

Especially note things such as participation grades, or grades for turning in all homework. Often, one can pick up 10% of their grade by just participating in class (or lose 10% by staring at the floor). Every serious student should get the full 10%.

Same with homework. If a professor gives 10% for just turning in homework each class, such as exercises in a foreign language workbook, then make *sure* you turn something in. Get that full 10% every single time. Do not falter. These things are freebies and you must take advantage of them without exception. No excuses.

Some professors give a percentage for e-mailing a short analysis of something to him/her before class, such as an analysis of a poem in a literature class, or by answering some questions the professor has already posed. From the beginning, get in the habit of doing these things and don't miss a one, ever.

It is critical to know where to put one's emphasis in a course, whether on the research paper for the semester, exams, or something else. Analyze the syllabus thoroughly and know where you are going. Don't be blind and in the dark. There is no excuse for it.

Even mediocre students will benefit enormously by knowing what counts what, and having a plan.

6. Note whether you can earn extra credit.

If you can, DO IT. Always do it. Whether it's attend a series of lectures, write an extra paper or go to a play, just do it. The more cushion one can get in any course during the semester, the better, and professors are invariably impressed by students who do extra work.

Always be thinking this way.

7. Make sure you buy ALL your school books for the semester, the sooner the better.

Buy them in the summer before the fall semester starts.

Buy them the moment the book store opens after Christmas before the spring semester starts. Buying early guarantees the bookstore won't be out.

Buy all workbooks or manuals, star charts, study guides and any additional material suggested by a professor. Like a carpenter whose tools are his hammer and saw, these are your tools and they will help you. Just having them will give you confidence.

8. Make sure you have a dictionary, thesaurus and other personal reference books unique to your field.

Don't skimp. Buy the reference books you need immediately. They will pale in price to your course books and you can use them the whole time you are in school, then into graduate school or life.

If you need to subscribe to something, do it. If you need *501 Latin Verbs*, go buy it. Be a serious student. Ask your professors which reference books you should get.

Good examples of reference books unique to your field are a history fact-finder if you are a History major, or a rhyming dictionary if you are studying poetry and need to write some.

9. It's good to have a desktop encyclopedia, though a Google search of any topic will usually turn up several good sources such as Wikipedia.

Anytime you search online, make sure several credible websites are saying the same thing before you believe it. Always double-check Wikipedia.

Encyclopedic entries are always good starting points for deeper research. Look at the bibliography or sources cited in any encyclopedia article. You may want to examine some of those sources.

10. During the semester, CliffsNotes®, SparkNotes® or an equivalent study guide WILL come in handy.

Don't hesitate a second to use CliffsNotes, SparkNotes or their equivalent – not as a substitute for reading the assignment – but because they have additional information that is excellent and extremely valuable and will help you enormously.

For example, the CliffsNotes booklet *Beowulf*,[2] in the Table of Contents, lists chapters: "Life and Background of the Poet," "Introduction to Beowulf," "Critical Commentaries," "Character Analyses," "Critical Essays," then has questions you can answer. This is outstanding material to have at your fingertips and refer back to as you pore over the assignment.

11. Many study guides are not just literary.

CliffsNotes, for example, covers writing,

---

[2] *Beowulf*, CliffsNotes, Stanley P. Baldwin, Author, (Foster City, CA: IDG Books Worldwide, Inc., 2000).

foreign languages, math, sciences, business and economics, history, political science, test preparation and more.

Do a Google search to see what's out there. Go to their websites and see what is available. There might be a beneficial paper in PDF format you can buy and download.

Just make SURE you never plagiarize or turn something in as your own that you found somewhere. You can have your college career destroyed by doing so and you would deserve it. Professors, nowadays, know how to catch you copying from the Internet so don't even think about it. You can't learn by doing that anyway!

12. You might want to create your own study aid in a course by copying the glossary or other material in the back of a book.

You, then, will have it on your desk at your fingertips without having to pick up the book and go to the end; and you can tag it, write on it, underline things, etc.

Think this way, and create custom tools to help you save time and excel.

13. Include, as one of your reference books, *The Elements of Style* by William Strunk, Jr. and E. B. White.

This legendary little book has been around for

a century. It was written by Cornell University English professor, William Strunk, Jr., for his students in 1918, but it has been updated over the years and made relevant for today. It is a vital piece of work and extremely valuable for any student or professional. Here is a powerful excerpt:

> Omit needless words.
> Vigorous writing is concise. A sentence should contain no unnecessary words, a paragraph no unnecessary sentences, for the same reason that a drawing should have no unnecessary lines and a machine no unnecessary parts. This requires not that the writer make all sentences short, or avoid all detail and treat subjects only in outline, but that every word tell.[3]

14. **Writing is a critical skill for ALL students and for people in the workforce. Read E. B. White's essay on writing in** *The Elements of Style*: **"An Approach to Style (With a List of Reminders)." It is outstanding!**

E. B. White was a student of Professor Strunk at Cornell. He wrote several books in his life but

---

[3] William Strunk, Jr. and E. B. White, *The Elements of Style*, Fourth Edition (New York: Longman, 2000), 23.

is best known for the famous children's books, *Charlotte's Web* and *Stuart Little*. He was an esteemed writer for *The New Yorker* magazine during its heyday and contributed to it for 60 years. White revised *The Elements of Style* in 1959, the second edition in 1972 and the third in 1979.

Here's an excerpt from White's "An Approach to Style (With a List of Reminders)":

> Who can confidently say what ignites a certain combination of words, causing them to explode in the mind? Who knows why certain notes in music are capable of stirring the listener deeply, though the same notes slightly rearranged are impotent?... The preceding chapters [in *The Elements of Style*] contain instructions drawn from established English usage; this one contains advice drawn from a writer's experience of writing.[4]

Purchase the most current edition of *The Elements of Style* (fourth, as of 2012) and read it, or at least glance over it as soon as you can.

---

[4] E. B. White, "An Approach to Style (With a List of Reminders)" in *The Elements of Style*, Strunk and White, Fourth Edition (see note 3), 66.

This book, *The Elements of Academic Success*, is inspired by, and formatted like *The Elements of Style*, with its bold topic sentences followed by one or more paragraphs of discussion.

15. Two other EXCELLENT books on writing will help you enormously.

The first is Stephen King's *On Writing, A Memoir of the Craft*. It is a classic that is EASY to read. You will absorb an incredible amount of important information from the horror master.

The second is William Zinsser's *On Writing Well, The Classic Guide to Writing Nonfiction*. The *Library Journal,* on the back cover of *On Writing Well,* says "Not since *The Elements of Style* has there been a guide to writing as well presented and readable as this one. A love and respect for the language is evident on every page."[5]

You can get these books cheaply from Amazon or other places online, or at any large bookstore.

You don't have to read them cover to cover (although you will probably want to). Just read what interests you, or what you feel you need. They are both FULL of dynamic information on writing that will put you WORLDS ahead of other

---

[5] William Zinsser, *On Writing Well, The Classic Guide to Writing Nonfiction,* 30th Anniversary Edition, Seventh Edition (New York: Collins, 2006).

students and people in the workforce.

16. An excerpt from Stephen King's *On Writing*.

Stephen King writes:

> You might also notice how much simpler the thought is to understand when it's broken up into two thoughts. This makes matters easier for the reader, and the reader must always be your main concern; without Constant Reader, you are just a voice quacking in the void. And it's no walk in the park being the guy on the receiving end. '[Will Strunk] felt the reader was in serious trouble most of the time,' E. B. White writes in his introduction to *The Elements of Style*, 'a man floundering in a swamp, and that it was the duty of anyone trying to write English to drain this swamp quickly and get his man up on dry ground, or at least throw him a rope.' And remember: **The writer threw the rope**, not

The rope was thrown by the writer.
Please oh please.[6]

The emphasis is King's.

17. Short excerpts from William Zinsser's
On Writing Well.

William Zinsser writes:

> Writing is hard work. A clear
> sentence is no accident. Very few
> sentences come out right the first
> time, or even the third time.
> Remember this in moments of
> despair. If you find that writing is
> hard, it's because it *is* hard.
> (emphasis is Zinsser's).[7]

And:

> Enthusiasm is the force that keeps
> you going and keeps the reader in
> your grip. When your zest begins to
> ebb, the reader is the first person to
> know it.[8]

---

[6] Stephen King, *On Writing, A Memoir of the Craft*
(New York: Pocket Books, 2000), 124.
[7] Zinsser, *On Writing Well,* 9.
[8] Ibid., 52.

And:

> Use active verbs unless there is no
> comfortable way to get around using
> a passive verb. The difference
> between an active-verb style and a
> passive-verb style – in clarity and
> vigor – is the difference between life
> and death for a writer.[9]

18. Use only notebooks with a pocket in the front. One-subject notebooks are best.

Put your syllabus in the pocket so you always have it close at hand. Any important changes a professor gives you over the semester, such as a new exam date or study-session date, or new date for the first draft of a paper, you will be able to record immediately directly onto your syllabus, and you will know exactly where it is.

Also, you will accumulate handouts in most classes during the semester. Keep them all in one place, in that course's notebook pocket.

One subject notebooks are best because multiple-subject notebooks get bulky and some only have one pocket. There is no way you can keep all the handouts and returned tests for a semester for three courses in a single pocket. Even one pocket for one course fills up!

---

[9] Ibid., 67.

It is extremely important and helpful to keep everything for a course - from syllabus to returned tests to handouts and anything else - in the course's notebook pocket. That way you absolutely know where everything related to that course is located at all times.

19. Make sure somebody can find you to return a lost notebook.

Write you name, of course, and vital information like cell phone number and e-mail address, but also write the course title, place it meets and when, and professor's name. Give somebody a chance to find you and get your lost notebook back to you. You don't EVER want to lose a notebook.

If you fill up a notebook, get another one, even if it is late in the semester.

Use different notebook colors so you can easily identify which course a notebook is for.

20. Put all of your school materials in one place in your room or house.

Make it easy on yourself. Keep all of your school related things in one place inside your house, apartment, dorm room or wherever you live, so you know where everything is and can go right to anything. Backpack, books, notebooks, everything. It will save you a lot of time otherwise spent looking around your apartment for some class assignment sheet. It will guarantee that nothing ever gets lost, and it will save time when you are late and rushing out the door to class. You'll be able to grab exactly what you need and take off.

21. Find your college library and other libraries in your area that you can use.

Find *every* library in the area that you have access to, such as the public library, and any other college's library for which your college might have a reciprocal borrowing agreement. Often, if a book is checked out of your school's library, you can find it across town.

If you can't find a book locally, try to find it online. The online book world (Amazon, AbeBooks, Alibris, et al.) is extremely competitive and prices for used books in good condition often start at a penny.

22. Libraries are EXTREMELY valuable assets.

Check out their web sites for research tips, electronic journals, encyclopedias, databases, etc., that you can access from your computer at home. Each library has specialized reference books you can use, and each has reference librarians who are more than willing to help.

Make friends with EVERYBODY who works in any library, especially reference librarians. Smile and say hello. Abide by the rules on being quiet. Speak to them on the street. Drink a beer with them if you see them at a bar. If you do this, they will go OUT of their way to help you when you ask for it.

I've always been good friends with everybody in the College of Charleston library. Ran into a friend, James, head of circulation at the time, during the beginning of the Cooper River Bridge Run years ago with 30,000 other runners mulling around. We talked excitedly about the race, and bonded, and every time we saw each other after that, we were Bridge-running brothers. There is nothing he wouldn't go out of his way to help me with in that library.

23. Walk into a library and feel the power, knowledge, art, culture, history, literature, and science stored there.

Let it overwhelm you (but don't act like you're having a seizure in the lobby).

Libraries are sacred places.

Go to the library to study. It is quiet and there are always cubbyholes and corners you can hole-up in.

Another thing that is great about the library: potential love interests are always there and you can check them out too.

24. Don't hesitate to ask a reference librarian a question, or use interlibrary loan.

Reference librarians can save you a ton of time and are glad to help.

Don't hesitate to use interlibrary loan, which is when you access the catalog of another library somewhere and request to borrow one of their books. Your library must process the request for you, and nowadays, interlibrary loan requests are filled fast and the system easy to use. You will then have the power of most other libraries in America at your fingertips. Your public library can also process inter-library loan requests.

25. When you go to the stacks to look for a book, remember, there are likely several other books around that book on the same topic.

Examine them too. Sit down on the floor and go through the whole section thoroughly.

26. Always carry change and some dollars in your backpack in case you need to make copies.

Don't hesitate to make copies of *anything* that might help you later. You will need to cite your sources. Just make a copy of the page or two of publishing and copyright information in the front of any book, and same for a periodical including volume information, month, etc.

With newspaper articles, make sure the newspaper's name and city, section of the paper, article title, date, and reporter's name, if given, are included.

Just make sure you have ALL the information you might need to property cite your source.

27. Make copies of *every* article you are supposed to read, so you own them.

Don't just go to the library and temporarily check out a reserve article and read it then turn it back in. Be a serious student! Make a copy of the article then devour it, write all over it, highlight things, tag things, have it at your fingertips, refer back to it, and keep it for future reference.

28. Do all your copying for the semester at one time, if possible.

It is highly efficient to block out an afternoon or two at the beginning of the semester and make copies of *all* the articles you will need for the semester such as periodicals on reserve at the library, etc.

This is much more efficient than running to the library one article at a time.

It's like fueling your car. You can hassle with stopping twice a week for a few gallons, or stop once every three weeks and fill it up.

Which is more efficient: Six wasteful stops at the gas station, or one?

Some articles won't be posted or available. You can get those later.

Anything you can't get right away, write the title on the front page of your calendar, and write it on a sticky note and stick it on the front of your notebook so it is in your face until you can get it.

29. If you can't do a whole semester's worth of copying and downloading, then do half the semester.

If that doesn't work, do it every month or every two weeks. The point is to get AHEAD of the game without having to constantly scramble, and it is good to look at material and assignments in advance and have them on your mind.

Mark your calendar to let you know in advance when you must do the next two weeks, or the next month's copying and downloading.

30. Whatever you do, don't wait until the last minute to make copies or read something.

Have needed materials at your fingertips. You will get little out of an article you rushed through at the library the day it is due, but on the other hand, if you own the article, you can make it part of your extended brainpower and you can refer back to it, especially before an exam.

Anything you can't copy right then, make a note of it on your calendar and on a sticky-note stuck to the front of your notebook, so you can get it copied and read in plenty of time for the assignment.

31. You need a computer with Internet access, and a printer.

A computer and printer are essential. Prices have come way down.

If you still can't afford one, get on Craigslist and talk somebody down to $25 for an old one. Windows XP is still a good operating system.

Buy as much computer as you can.

Get the fastest Internet connection you can, usually DSL or broadband. It will save a ton of time in the long run and it's definitely worth it.

If you, somehow, still can't get a computer, find out where you can use one. Your school or library should have a computer center somewhere, where students can use computers, get on the Internet and print.

32. Electrical surge protection and virus protection for your computer are critical.

Your computer should always be on a UPS (Uninterrupted Power Supply) to protect from regular electrical surges and spikes in home electricity, and surges from an outside source such as lightning. Most of these systems are made up of batteries that are trickle-charged when you plug the UPS into your wall.

You plug your computer, monitor, sometimes phone lines, and other electronic items, into the UPS. If your electricity goes off, the UPS will continue to power your electronics for a short period of time so you can save your work and turn off your computer in the normal way.

Do some research. UPSs are not that expensive these days. Definitely protect your computer, which means you are also protecting your schoolwork that is on that computer!

Protect your computer from viruses too. You can pick up a virus or other malware from anywhere – e-mail, a download, a website, etc. – and some viruses can wipe you out. Definitely use virus software. If you can't afford Norton or McAfee, then try Microsoft's free virus protection: Security Essentials. It's pretty good, and certainly better than nothing.

33. If a course has material on the Internet, bookmark the website early on.

If a course has a web site, or your professor has course information on his/her web site, then go to it as soon as you can and bookmark it.

Also, write the web address inside the front

cover of your course notebook.

34. Create a master directory (folder) on your computer for the semester. Here's what to do using Windows *(Apple people please follow same procedures using Apple protocol).*

Look in Libraries and find "Documents" (or "My Documents") and double-click.

After double-clicking on Documents, you are inside Documents. You can see all the other folders that are inside your Documents.

You can change the way your folders and files look on the screen if you want to. Just put your cursor in the My Documents area, right-click and choose "View." You'll see eight options. I like the "Large icons" view, but you do what you want.

Right-click in that same area again and the same menu that includes "View" will pop up again.

This time choose "New," and another menu will pop up and one of your options will be "Folder."

Click on Folder. A new folder will be created.

A folder and a directory are the same thing (going forward, I will use FOLDER only).

The place where you type in the name of the folder will be highlighted so you can type in a name. Type in the name of your school and date, or whatever title you want for your master folder. As an example, I'm going to demonstrate a master

folder by entitling mine: College of Charleston –
Fall, 2013.

35. Create folders INSIDE your master folder for your individual courses.

Double-click on your master folder, College of
Charleston – Fall, 2013. That will put you inside
the folder College of Charleston – Fall, 2013.

Right-click and choose New then Folder (just
as you did above) then type in the name of your
first course e.g., Astronomy 101.

Follow the same procedure to create your
other four course folders e.g.: History 101, English
101, Political Science 101, and Spanish 101.

This is a typical freshman first semester.

36. Create additional folders inside your course folders if you want to.

You might have a paper and presentation in a
course such as History 101. In the History 101
folder, you might want to create a folder and
name it "Paper," and create another and name it
"Presentation," and save various things to each.

You can do this any way you want. Do what is
comfortable for you. Do what helps you organize
your material and put it at your fingertips.

37. You don't have to put your master folder in Documents.

You can put it on any hard drive or anywhere else, but Documents is a perfect place for it.

When you double-click on Documents in the future, you will see all the folders in Documents including College of Charleston – Fall, 2013.

When you double-click on College of Charleston – Fall, 2013, you will see your five course folders: Astronomy 101, History 101, English 101, Political Science 101, and Spanish 101.

Double-click any one of them to go inside that folder so you can save files belonging to that course, and see any other folders within that folder.

38. If you want your master folder to appear first, in Documents, or earlier than its alphabetization would allow, then simply put a 0 or 1 in front of the folder name.

When you double-click on Documents, all the folders in Documents appear, and they are alphabetized. The computer places numerals before letters in alphabetization. To make your master folder the first one in your Documents, or in the first few folders, simple add a 0 or 1 in front of the name. Your master folder would then be: 1 College of Charleston – Fall, 2013.

39. You can change the name of any folder or file at any time, easily.

Just click on the folder or file, so that it is highlighted, then click again, and the folder or file name will be highlighted. You can then type in anything you want. You can modify the current name or put in a completely different name.

In essence, you are clicking twice but you are NOT double-clicking. Double-clicking is a rapid two clicks. Clicking twice is slow with maybe a second or two between clicks.

If you click too fast, you will have double-clicked, and you end up inside the folder, and will have to go back a step.

40. Download everything for the semester at one time, if possible.

Not only will you be able to see what kind of things you will be studying, but more importantly, you'll have everything at your fingertips. You won't have to worry about a professor's server being down or Internet connection problems at 2 a.m. the day of a test when you need to download a study guide and cram.

41. Save your downloaded files in the appropriate course folder.

Do this by downloading the file so it is open on

your computer. It might be a PDF (Portable Document Format) file since they are widespead and an excellent format.

With PDF files, just move your cursor to the bottom of the screen and some options will appear. The one on the far left is an image of floppy disk. We don't use floppy disks that much any more but once upon a time, that's all we used. The graphic still represents saving your file.

Click on the floppy disk and a menu will pop up with "Save As" at the top and just below it, "Save In."

Find the folder you want to save in and click on it once to highlight it, or double-click so you are inside it, then hit Save.

If you have downloaded a Word file (.doc), you might have to double-click on the file name so that it opens in Word or a word processing program, then look at the top menu bar and click "File," then in the pull-down box click "Save as," then fill in a file name.

Make *sure* you save to the correct course folder. That information will be on your left. You will see Libraries and under it, Documents.

Double-click on Documents and you will see your master folder, College of Charleston – Fall, 2013.

Double-click on it, and you will see all your course folders.

Double-click on the appropriate course folder,

then, when you save your file, it will be saved in that folder.

All this might seem like a lot but it is a piece of cake after you have saved a few things. You HAVE to know how to do all this to operate in today's computerized world.

42. Here's a link to some good information on files and folders from Microsoft. I'm sure Apple has similar information easily accessible.

Go to www.Windows.Microsoft.com. In the top right, there is a rectangle, and if you place the cursor over it, it says "Search this website." Type in "files and folders" (without quotation marks).[10]

It will instantly give you several links.

On the left are several operating systems under heading "Filter by Product." They include Windows 8 Release Preview, Windows 7, Windows Vista and Windows XP. Click on your operating system and you will be given specific links to file and folder information for your operating system.

Much of the information on files and folders is the same for all operating systems but definitely go to your exact operating system such as Windows 7, just to be safe.

You can also do a Google search for "files and

---

[10] Information on files and folders from Microsoft, accessed March 25, 2013, http://www.Windows.Microsoft.com, then search for "files and folders."

folders" and a lot of good information will pop up.

43. Make a backup copy of your master folder on a flash drive.

It's IMPERATIVE that you backup your master folder to a flash drive or other external drive. That way, if your computer breaks, or crashes, or your main hard drive goes out, you still have all your work on a flash drive.

In fact, back it up to TWO flash drives if you can. You are talking about your whole semester's work! You might have a paper you have been working on for weeks stored in a course folder. If you lose that paper, you are dead.

Some of your final exams will be cumulative. You'll want to make sure you have all previous handouts and documents safe and sound, so you can study them for your final.

44. It's easy to make a copy of your master folder.

Using the example above, in which we named our master folder College of Charleston – Fall, 2013, just click on Documents, and when you see College of Charleston – Fall, 2013, then click on it once, so that it is highlighted.

Put your cursor over the highlighted folder and right-click.

A menu will appear and one of your options

will be "Copy." Click on it.

Then, go to whatever drive you want to put your backup copy on. Say you have a flash drive that your system recognizes as Drive E.

Double-click on Drive E so that you are in Drive E. You'll see on the screen all the folders on your Drive E. Put your cursor on the screen with the other folders (but don't highlight any!) and right-click.

A menu will pop up and one of the options will be "Paste." Click on it.

The moment you do, a copy of College of Charleston – Fall, 2013 will be put on your Drive E and take its place with the other folders on Drive E.

Make sure, before you click on Paste, that no folder is highlighted. Otherwise, your copy of College of Charleston – Fall, 2013 will go in that folder.

45. Always create TWO files of anything you are working on in case you accidentally delete the main one, or the main one becomes corrupted. Here's an easy way to do it.

Say you are working on a paper for a Shakespeare class using MS Word or some other word processor. You might name your file: Shakespeare301Paper.doc.

Now, ALSO save it as Shakespeare301Paper-BACKUP.doc.

It's so easy and you always have two files and that is important. Files get corrupted, or you can mess them up yourself easy enough.

The best way to follow this method is to do this: Save the main file –
Shakespeare301Paper.doc – then click File, and Save As.

The file name you just saved –
Shakespeare301Paper – should still be right there in front of you, and highlighted. If it's not, type it in.

Click behind Shakespeare301Paper so that you can add to the file name, then add the dash and BACKUP. I like putting BACKUP in caps because it makes the backup file stand out.

Then click Save, and you are done. You will now have two identical files:
Shakespeare301Paper.doc *and*
Shakespeare301Paper-BACKUP.doc. (the file name suffix, such as .doc, is added automatically by Word and other word processors).

If an evil computer gremlin corrupts your Shakespeare301Paper.doc file, all you have to do is open Shakespeare301Paper-BACKUP.doc, then click File, Save as, and save it as Shakespeare301Paper.doc, which was your original file before the gremlin got it.

You would then have restored your main Shakespeare paper file, and be back to having two perfect files.

If you did not have a backup, you would be DEAD. Your Shakespeare paper file would be gone and you would be up you-know-what creek without a paddle.

46. Save individual files you are working on to both your master folder AND the master folder backup on your flash drive.

Save your files *frequently* as you work. I used plural – files – because you should be saving *two* files every time you save. Remember the example above: Shakespeare301Paper.doc *and* Shakespeare301Paper-BACKUP.doc.

ALWAYS do this.

At the end of your work session, after you have saved both files for the last time, change the folder you are saving to — to your master folder backup on your flash drive, and save both files there.

OR, you can copy both files from your master folder in My Documents, to the master folder on your flash drive

Whatever you do, it's BEST to have a rigid routine when it comes to saving and backing up your work. ALWAYS think about what you are doing and be conscious of what you are doing! It is incredibly easy to copy an old file over a new one, and if you do that, you wipe out all your work for that day, or worse.

47. Also back up your work to a CD or DVD, something that is separate from your computer in case your computer blows up.

If your house takes a direct lighting strike, even a UPS might not save your computer, and you could lose even backups on flash drives.

Copy your master folder to a CD or DVD regularly, then remove the CD or DVD from the computer. Put it in a protective plastic CD case.

You can also copy your master folder to an extra flash drive or two, then remove them. That will give you another layer of protection.

48. Consider subscribing to a service that backs up your files automatically.

Do some research. One service recommended by Kim Komando is www.Carbonite.com, but there are others.[11]

49. BE EXTREMELY CAREFUL when copying files and folders. You can destroy all your work if you aren't.

Make SURE you don't copy an old file over a new one. That's why I put "BACKUP" in caps.

When you start working each day, just make

---

[11] Carbonite, automatic online file backup service suggested by Kim Komando, accessed March 25, 2013, http://www.Carbonite.com

sure you start with a file in your master folder in My Documents. You might need to go to a course folder in your master folder. As long as you always start in My Documents, you can rest assured that your most current work is always in your master folder in My Documents.

50. A deleted file will stay in your Recycle Bin until you use the "Empty the Recycle Bin" command.

A deleted file is stored in your Recycle Bin in case you need to restore it from there, but don't depend on your Recycle Bin for anything. It is a last ditch save option.

As stated, always make two copies, at least, of every important file AND save them to your master folder AND your backup master folder.

51. All of the above ideas for backing up files and folders are outstanding, but develop your own.

You can adopt any of my systems as they are, you can modify them and adopt the hybrid or create something new. It's best if you do what is comfortable for you. You'll remember to do it regularly, as you should, because it will be your system.

Just do whatever will guarantee that you save your files, regularly, with multiple names and in as many different places as you can. That is the ONLY way to protect your critical work.

52. It's a good idea to print, every so often, a paper or other assignment you are working on.

Print your work, even if it is an early rough draft. If there was a catastrophe and you lost all your computer files and backups, you would still have that printout to start all over with.

Better safe than sorry, ALWAYS!

II
Professors

Most professors are decent people who enjoy teaching their material and really want you to succeed in their classes, but some are unquestionably better than others, and some are unquestionably harder graders than others. You'll have to decide the best fit for you.

53. Professors are people too!

It is unquestionably in a student's best interest to earn the respect of his or her professors, and, even better, be liked by their professors.

Professors are gods in their classrooms with the power of life or death over grades, but professors are people too! They each have personal interests, passions, family, a favorite team and at least one dear alma mater.

Now, a professor is going to like a student who shows up on time, is prepared, participates in class discussions, does not chew gum, wear a hat, drink water, eat, crinkle paper or sleep. That's just common sense and basic courtesy.

But, you can go beyond that, and should.

54. Do some research on your professors.

Go to their departmental home pages and read their curricula vitae. Go to their personal websites and blogs. Find out where they went to school, what kind of degrees they have, articles they have published or books written. Do Google searches on your professors.

During the semester, professors will mention something important to them about their good old days in graduate school, or teaching here or there, or some book they have written. Make a note of it and ask them about it later. It's just basic human nature for a professor to like someone who shows an interest in their beloved field of study, or some important accomplishment.

And it's not "sucking up" to show professors that you appreciate them enough to know something about them. It's smart, and you will learn something in the process. It's the same way in the working world. It's good to know something about people with whom one is doing business.

55. You might be impressed with your professors' accomplishments.

A good number of professors are well-respected in their fields, appear on TV and in the newspaper as experts, are sought-after lecturers around town and have written numerous articles and books. It is good to know all this.

56. One day you might need letters of recommendation for graduate school or for scholarships and grants, or you might need references in the working world.

If you have worked hard and participated in a professor's class, especially if you made an "A" and did extra work, a professor will likely be glad to write a good letter of recommendation for you or give you a glowing personal reference. And even more so if he/she likes you.

57. Grading is subjective, especially on essay and discussion exams, so think about this.

To graduate magna cum laude, you need to go for "A"s in every course. If you are in a course and an A is 90 to 100 and you have an 89.3 average, you better hope you have impressed your professor enough that he/she might just decide you deserve an A.

Or, if you are close to making an A, you might be able to persuade your professor to let you do an extra credit assignment that will tip the scale and get you your A. It can and does happen.

Of course, if you need a C to graduate, and a C is 70 to 80, and your average is 69.3, it is even *more* critical that you have a good relationship with your professor. You probably will have to suck up and beg, but you will be much better off by knowing something about your professor and having a good relationship with him or her.

No matter what, you'll have lots of professors. You'll have to deal with all of them. Make it a positive experience every time.

58. Though professors are people too, always use your head.

A classroom is a place of intellectual inquiry and most professors encourage vigorous debate no matter what one's convictions or position taken during a discussion. Argue as forcefully as you'd like, but use common sense and be polite. Always be cool.

If you think a professor is the worse S.O.B. who ever tread a classroom, hold that thought until your anonymous evaluation at the end of the semester then let the professor have it with both barrels. An administrator in the department will likely compile all the anonymous student comments for the professor and department head to read, and they do read them. You are doing the school, department head and professor a big favor by writing an honest evaluation of the professor's performance. They need feedback just like we all do, and the best ones crave it.

If you simply can not deal with a professor, by all means, drop the course. Take it under a different professor, or take a different course.

59. Not all professors are good professors.

Most professors are wonderful teachers and purveyors of knowledge who are interesting and enlightened, but there are some who STINK. Some are too ideological or are politically correct. Some are mediocre teachers. Some are boring lecturers. Some don't grade fairly.

If any of these complaints apply to you, suffer through the semester and do the best you can, then let the professor have it between the eyes on the anonymous evaluation.

Also, report them on RateMyProfessors.com so other students can be forewarned.[12]

Make sure you also report the outstanding professors and the good things about them too!

Most of the time, one can learn something from any professor. Look for the positive.

60. Academia is clearly liberal. Over 80% of professors are liberals and most are Democrats. It is an indisputable fact of college life.

It has been well-known and documented for

---

[12] RateMyProfessors is an outstanding website for evaluating college professors, accessed March 25, 2013, http://www.RateMyProfessors.com.

over 40 years that the news media and academia are overwhelmingly liberal. It is a solid FACT. Do a Google search for "liberal bias in academia" or "liberal bias in the news media" and study after study, article after article, will pop up.

Just be aware of it. It is not the best situation for vigorous intellectual debate and a diversity of ideas, but it is what it is. Liberals hire their own and promote their own.

Often, if there is a difference of opinion among faculty members, non-liberals do not speak up. If they do, they risk not getting tenure.

61. More than likely, a professor's liberal ideology is not going to be a problem because professors know there are twice as many conservatives in the county as liberals.

A recent Gallup Poll confirms it. In an article on Gallup's website dated January 12, 2012 entitled "Conservatives Remain the Largest Ideological Group in U.S.," Gallup writes: "Political ideology in the U.S. held steady in 2011, with 40% of Americans continuing to describe their views as conservative, 35% as moderate, and 21% as liberal. This marks the third straight year that conservatives have outnumbered moderates, after more than a decade in which moderates mainly tied or outnumbered conservatives."[13]

Liberal professors know our country is a center/right, moderate/conservative country, and not liberal, and most professors know that the classroom is supposed to be a place of open, unlimited inquiry, and not indoctrination.

62. Liberal bias sneaks in constantly, so be aware.

A good example happened in a political science class I took one time. The professor was a big-city northeastern liberal and admitted it, but was a good guy and fair in class. He did encourage everybody to say whatever they wanted.

However, when discussing non-profit political organizations, he quoted a list of several as if those were the best ones in the country, and every one was hard left liberal, either anti-Second Amendment, pro-labor union, pro-choice, radical environmentalist, anti-capitalism, etc. By bringing up only those organizations, it planted them in the minds of some students as the only ones worthwhile, which is not the case at all.

This is a benign example of liberal bias in the classroom but it is worth noting for the stealthy

---

[13] "Conservatives Remain the Largest Ideological Group in U.S.", article on Gallup website by Lydia Saad dated January 12, 2012 based on a Gallup Poll, accessed March 25, 2013, http://www.gallup.com/poll/152021/ conservatives-remain-largest-ideological-group.aspx.

method used. Real bias does exist and can be much more dangerous and unfair.

When the standard for judging all other ideas is hard left liberal, one will unquestionably get a slanted, biased view and incorrect analysis.

But usually, at the very worst, you'll only have to suffer through boring lectures or comments in class.

And again, if the professor is so liberal that your suffering is unbearable, drop the class and take it with a better professor, or take a different course.

63. "Word of mouth" about professors: take it with a grain of salt.

Just because somebody says a professor is boring or hard, or even easy, don't take their word for it. Everybody is different. I have adored professors that others said were a drag.

However, if a lot of people say the same thing, then, there might be some truth to it, good or bad.

Most professors are decent people who enjoy teaching their material and really want you to succeed in their classes, but some are unquestionably better than others, and some are unquestionably harder graders than others. You'll have to decide the best fit for you.

64. Definitely use RateMyProfessors.com.

The popularity and success of the website, RateMyProfessors.com is undeniable! It's a fun site that is extremely helpful and easy to use.[14]

Professors are rated on a one-to-five scale in three main categories: Helpfulness, Clarity and Easiness.

There is an average rating for each of the categories and an overall quality rating. Also, the total number of students rating a professor is listed, and by each individual rating there are usually comments up to four sentences long. The comments are extremely valuable!

And just for fun, there is a Hotness indicator for good-looking professors signified by a red hot chili pepper.

If a professor has a lot of ratings posted and his/her averages are high on the 1-5 scale, that's a good sign; but it doesn't necessarily mean a professor with lower averages is not as good a

---

[14] The "About RateMyProfessors.com" section of the RateMyProfessors website states: "RateMyProfessors.com is the largest online destination for professor ratings. With 8,000 schools and over 15 million entirely student-generated comments and ratings, RateMyProfessors.com is the highest trafficked free site for quickly researching and rating 1.7 million professors from colleges and universities across the United States, Canada, and the United Kingdom. Over 4 million college students each month are using RateMyProfessors – join the fun!", accessed March 25, 2013, http://www.RateMyProfessors.com/About.jsp.

professor. All it takes are a couple lazy sour-grape students to give a good professor low marks, and that professor's average will fall.

65. Most student comments on RateMyProfessors.com are very sincere.

And 65% are positive, according to the Rate My Professors Team. It is easy to tell which comments are sour grapes written by students who were slackers. The site is clearly not dominated by angry students taking their wrath out on professors. It is, overall, a very thoughtful, sincere site that encourages truth and fair evaluation of professors.

66. Use common sense with RateMyProfessors.com.

If there are only a few ratings, then don't pay much attention to them. But once a professor has 10 or more ratings, you can usually see a pattern in the comments and that's what you are looking for. You want to see the same things repeated over and over, good or bad. You can give those things credibility after a while. If a professor has 10 ratings and all 10 state that he/she is boring as hell, or outstanding, then he/she probably is.

Also, poorly written comments with misspelled words should be disregarded or given less credibility.

67. It's almost a good idea to disregard the overall averages and concentrate on the comments.

However, professors with exceptionally high or exceptionally low average scores, probably are exceptionally good, or exceptionally not-so-good, professors.

Also, be aware that *all* the courses a professor has taught are included in the average score, meaning a professor can have ratings on 100-level freshman courses mixed in with ratings on 700-level graduate courses, and everything in between.

A professor might not be as good with 100-level incoming freshmen as he/she is with graduate students in the professor's specialty, or vice versa. If you are a freshman or sophomore, pay attention to comments beside freshman and sophomore classes, but note all comments.

68. Be like a gold miner and mine the comments for gems of information.

If several comments say that meeting with a professor will usually get one a better grade, then do it! Find an opportunity to meet with a professor ASAP. It is always good to know your professor, anyway. Both you and the professor benefit, and you will stick out in a positive way in the professor's mind. They want to know that you care about the course!

69. There is an abundance of valuable course information in RateMyProfessors.com comments.

One might be able to compare the same course taught by different professors if enough comments are present.

If you plan on taking a certain course, review ALL the comments for that course. You'll see a lot of good information mentioned, from required readings, to tests, to the way the professor teaches and grades.

70. I researched most of my former professors and found the ratings and comments on RateMyProfessors.com accurate and reflective of my own experience.

It is good that professors are held accountable in a manner such as RateMyProfessors.com, though some will squeal like stuck-pigs about it.

The best professors could care less because they are concentrating on doing the best job teaching their courses. They know their evaluations will reflect the occasional disgruntled student.

In fact, RateMyProfessors.com is great feedback for professors! The best professors look at it that way and learn from it!

71. A good time to use RateMyProfessors.com is when you are registering for courses and know which professors are teaching what.

It's so easy to do a search on RateMyProfessors.com and find a particular professor then look at that professor's ratings and comments. It's almost irresponsible not to, because you need to match yourself up with the professor who will most likely help you meet your goals, whether it's because that professor is an easy grader, or a great professor, or something else.

RateMyProfessors.com is an extremely valuable tool, but use common sense and don't make it the final word because everybody is different. One's person's "boring" is another's "fascinating!" Look for the same things repeated over and over. Those things are probably true.

72. A course that includes a professor's specialty is going to be good.

A specialty is material the professor loves and may have loved since childhood! He/she might have done a dissertation or thesis on the topic. It is a labor of love to the professor, and that will come out in class.

Other courses, such as freshman English, might just be departmental obligations rather than labors of love, but even then, a good professor will fire up the class and make it a good course.

73. It is one of the delights of life to be in a class taught by a professor who adores the material.

Students can't help but get caught up in the professor's enthusiasm.

I had numerous outstanding professors at the College of Charleston. One was Dr. Joe Harrison, who taught me English 201. The man loved literature and you could tell with every word out of his mouth. He retired in 2006 with 69 total ratings on RateMyProfessors.com and an overall score of 4.8 out of 5.

Dr. Harrison was at the end of his career when I had him, short, thin, smiled a lot. The kind of person you liked immediately. I remember a discussion of Adonis and we were talking about Aphrodite trying to get Adonis sexually aroused, and Adonis was not paying attention to her. Dr. Harrison was saying that Adonis HAD to be a prepubescent kid or he would have been extremely excited by Aphrodite's attention: "No way he had any whiskers," said Dr. Harrison, "I mean, this is the GODDESS OF LOVE ... if he had ONE whisker he would have been all over her!"

Another one of my finest professors was

Dr. Susan Farrell. Every one of her classes was outstanding. She brought much knowledge, enthusiasm and love of material to each one.

Among her many published writings, Dr. Farrell wrote two 500-page books: *Critical Companion to Tim O'Brien*, and *Critical Companion to Kurt Vonnegut*.[15] I had courses under Dr. Farrell in which we read both of those authors.

We read Tim O'Brien in her 500-level *Vietnam War Literature* course. O'Brien is a Vietnam veteran who won the National Book Award for Fiction in 1979. I learned more about the Vietnam War in that course than in any history course I ever took.

You can imagine the discussions we had in those classes, led by a tough but nice professor with such tremendous knowledge and enthusiasm for the material.

It is good to know a professor's first love, and if you can take a course by a professor teaching his/her first love, you are in for a treat.

74. If you like a professor, take him/her as often as possible.

Go out of your way to get a professor you

---

[15] Susan Farrell, *Critical Companion to Tim O'Brien* (New York: Facts on File, 2011); *Critical Companion to Kurt Vonnegut* (New York: Facts on File, 2008).

really like and from whom you learn well. Get him/her to direct your independent study papers and projects.

It's good to have two or three courses with the same professor because he/she can give you a stronger letter of recommendation.

In fact, some professors won't give you a letter of recommendation if you have only had one course with him/her. The logic is that he/she doesn't know you and your work well enough to write a letter or recommendation.

Perhaps so, though I have had professors who only had me for one course, give a glowing letter of recommendation.

But after two courses, a professor does know you better, and if you aced both, it is likely that that professor will be glad to give you a good letter of recommendation or job reference.

75. Meet with your professor early in the semester if you expect the course to be difficult for you.

Make an appointment with your professor as soon as possible. Tell him/her that your goal is to make an "A" but you are concerned about so and so, then have a nice chat. Ask specific questions about things that count the most and how best to tackle them. Ask if he/she has a copy of an A paper, if a paper is required. Don't be pushy, of course, but GET the information you need to excel.

You can never go wrong doing this. Professors want you to excel. The professor will file a mental note away in his/her brain that you are a conscientious student who cares about the course. It will be an asset for you, then work hard and don't let your professor down!

76. If you disagree with a professor on an emotional issue, be prepared to suffer with anger or boredom.

For example, if you are adamantly pro-life, and know that a certain professor is adamantly pro-choice and known for talking about it all the time – or vice versa – don't take that professor's class unless you are prepared to suffer through comments and an attitude you despise. If you are that emotional about an issue, it might be too easy to get into a bad argument, and there will be a lot of days you leave angry or disgusted, or bottled-up.

77. Depending on how it's used, the term "dead white male" can be racist and derogatory.

The term "dead white male" allows some professors to put their political ideology ahead of the course they are teaching. Apparently, they are mocking the large number of white males in

Western history and literature, and implying that some kind of racial and gender quotas would have been better than what happened. Maybe they think that Shakespeare and Charles Dickens held minorities and women down, somehow. Sounds like plain old bigotry and political correctness to me.

These "enlightened" professors need to realize that they are demeaning the people about whom they are teaching. They are discrediting them, to a degree, and planting in students' minds that the accomplishments of these white males of past history and literature are tainted, somehow, because they are white and male. What else can one deduce when "dead white male" is used in a mocking, derisive, condescending way?

A professor could be attempting to be cool, but I can tell you that it bothers a LOT of students who come to college to study beloved literary figures, and many, perhaps most of whom, are white males.

I remember walking out of a graduate English class, one time, with a very bright young lady who was always eagerly answering questions and participating in class discussions. One could tell she loved literature and was highly motivated. She said, "I can't believe Dr. X's harping about dead white males. I came here because I LOVE everything written by those dead white males! I hate to hear that kind of CRAP." Actually, her word was a little more explicit.

78. Some professors think it is cutesy to pepper their lectures with "dead white male" this and "dead white male" that, but here's how I felt when I first heard it in a serious classroom.

I was in a graduate English course on the history and theory of rhetoric, and very excited about the topic. I was greatly looking forward to the course and had bought my book early and gone through it.

The arrogant professor, a young white woman, came sashaying in and said, in a condescending manner, that we'd mostly be studying "dead white males," then she smirked and added, "and most of them were gay."

My heart sank, not because of the "gay" comment, but because of her hateful, racist tone.

I was so disappointed.

I felt bad and hurt sitting there on the front row because I had really wanted to study this material and get into the course. I debated filing a racism complaint against her and I probably should have, but was so wrapped up in trying to graduate magna cum laude, I just didn't have the time.

Should she be belittling a towering figure in literature or philosophy simply because he was white and male? Should his contributions be lessened and tainted because he was white?

Where are we headed with this kind of thinking? What implications does it have for white people today? According to professors like this, white people are supposed to be ashamed of their ancestors, despite often huge contributions. I mean, she is teaching a rhetoric course dominated by deceased white males whether she likes it or not. If she doesn't like it, she ought to go teach something else.

79. It is perverse to taint the people you are teaching about because of their skin color as this rhetoric professor had done.

You can certainly criticize a person's work, life and place in history or literature, and that is fair; but to taint somebody solely because of skin color … well, that is racist.

Are we ever going to become a post-racial society in America? I think not with this kind of in-your-face racism, no matter how cute some think it might be.

It is so ironic that the very people who scream the loudest about racism are the most racist of all, whether they realize it or not. They see race in everything, everywhere. They USE race to their advantage.

I wondered what other bigotry this professor would inject into her teaching.

What's so funny, in a sort of sick way, is that

I'm sure this professor thought she was the height of enlightenment and open-mindedness. What a joke.

I dropped the course the next day and was very disappointed to have had to do so. Despite my high interest in the subject, there was no way I was going to endure that professor's bigoted anti-white, anti-heterosexual condescension all semester.

80. The standard for racism should be equally applied across the board.

If the term "dead white male" is used jokingly, then FINE, but to some professors it is part of their liberal race/class/gender ideology, and as such, is a racist insult to white people. In that context, it is no different from using the "n" word.

Can you imagine a professor railing against "dead black males" or "dead Hispanic males?" NO, because if he or she did, they would be buried up to their necks on the campus green and ridden over with a riding lawn mower!

81. The overwhelming majority of professors teach their material with great love and vigor, and leave politics out of it.

Or they are tolerant of others' beliefs.

But if you do end up despising a professor, by all mean, drop the course, and the sooner the

better, then report them on
RateMyProfessors.com, or take other action
against them.

82. If a course is not that important to you, then take the easiest professor.

If you are going to graduate magna cum
laude, you need to rack up some "A"s, and an easy
professor is money in the bank.

If you know that two professors are teaching
the same course, and one is a former department
head who gives essay exams, and the other, a new
professor who wants to be liked and gives
multiple-choice exams, take the multiple-choice
professor unless there is some compelling reason
why you should take the essay exam professor.

Perhaps you always do better on essay exams.
Or, perhaps you know and like the essay
professor, then, by all means, take him/her.

Otherwise, take the multiple-choice professor
and notch an A for the semester and don't feel
guilty. There will be plenty of hard courses up the
road that you will have to take, and you will have
no choice in who is teaching them.

83. If you screw up on your first test, go see your professor and tell him/her that you are going for an "A" in the course.

The best thing to do is not screw up, and show

your professor you want an A by doing superior work, by showing up prepared and on time, by participating in class discussions, doing all homework and making "A"s on exams and papers.

However, your first major grade in a course is critical and can set the tone for the entire semester. If you screw up and make a B or C, don't panic. Set up an appointment with your professor and go tell him/her that you are going for an A in the course and screwed up. Ask your professor's advice on how you can do better. Ask if there is any extra credit you can do. Be respectful, but let your determination come across.

You will undoubtedly impress your professor and show him/her that you care and are willing to work hard.

I know this is good advice because it happened to me. I made a C+ on the first test in Dr. Reynolds's *Cosmos in History* course and almost had a heart attack. I had studied in detail his time-line and that was the wrong thing to do.

From then on, I aced everything. And also, from then on, I was good friends with Dr. Reynolds and remained so the rest of his life.

Go see your professor and find out what to do, then do it.

84. Choose carefully the professor who will direct an important paper for you, such as for departmental honors.

It is probably best to choose somebody as close to your way of thinking, ideologically, as possible, to direct an important paper in a field such as History. Otherwise, you may find yourself at odds with historical interpretations, and a professor at odds with you will not encourage you to write what you want, or will discourage you from it because he/she thinks it is incorrect.

85. Professors who direct papers know that other professors often read those papers and NO professor wants something to end up in a paper that might make him/her look bad.

This is especially true about Southern history.

For example, if you want to write a paper on how economic factors dwarfed all other causes of the War Between the States, especially dwarfing the idea that slavery was the cause, then a professor who believes adamantly that slavery was the cause would not be a good person to direct your paper.

Of course, a good professor *should* let you argue what you want to argue, and just keep you on the scholarly path, but, sadly, it isn't always that way.

Just be careful who you get to direct

important papers. If you have any doubt about
your ability to work with a certain professor for
any reason, then don't. Find somebody better
suited to you.

86. If you are in a dispute with a professor, don't let him/her grade you.

Look for the opportunity to withdraw from the
course/paper with the right to do another with a
different faculty member; then find another
professor with whom you can work better.

If your grade on a paper is so important that a
poor one will prevent you from graduating magna
cum laude or with other honors, or prevent you
from achieving departmental honors, then,
whatever you do, do NOT let the professor grade
you.

There is a good chance that due to anger and
emotions you will get a lower grade than you
deserve, and you will NEVER be able to prove you
deserved a higher grade. A professor would be in a
position to use all of his/her ability as a scholar to
argue that you deserved a C+ and not the A you
needed. A professor could make any kind of case
against you, that you didn't provide enough
background, or adequately discuss all sides of an
issue, or anything else he/she chooses to argue.
Grading is so subjective that there is no judge on
earth capable of absolutely affirming that a paper

deserved a C+ instead of an A. The only thing a judge can say is that they would have given it a different grade, and for some other reason.

87. If you feel that you have been discriminated against by a professor, file a complaint.

All schools have a student handbook or something that outlines the procedure for filing a complaint against a professor. You can check with the undergraduate dean's office.

It is best, by far, to avoid a complete meltdown and confrontation, but sometimes it can't be helped. If you feel you are the victim of discrimination or some unfair action by a professor, then, by all means, file a complaint.

There is a good chance you will lose. No matter what, a professor, who is used to being a god and unchallenged, will have hard feelings.

88. The undergraduate dean's office will usually be genuinely sympathetic to a student's plight, and not automatically on the side of faculty.

In fact, the undergraduate dean can be a real advocate for a student unfairly treated by a faculty member.

If a panel of professors is assembled to hear the complaint of a student against a professor, the student will probably lose. It would be most unlikely a professor is going to go against another professor and set that kind of precedent. Not on a complaint that doesn't involve some huge issue for which attention is being placed on the school by the media. If it's just you against a professor, and he/she is being judged by their peers, you are probably going to lose.

However, you might be given, in the interest of fairness, some way out of the situation. For example, if you are having a dispute with a professor over a big paper he/she is directing, you might be allowed to withdraw from the course/paper and do another with a different faculty member.

89. I want to make it clear that it is always best to avoid a meltdown.

But in college, as in life, sometimes a meltdown happens and will require a showdown, especially if you feel your honor or a principle is involved. Discrimination does take place, and it happens against white people as well as blacks, Asians, Hispanics and everybody else.

If you feel like you have been discriminated against, then FIGHT. Go talk to an attorney to see if you have grounds for some kind of discrimination or civil rights law suit against the school.

Sometimes a law suit is the only way to solve a problem, in school as in life, though usually it should be the last resort.

90. A professor should stick by the syllabus

A syllabus is an important set of rules, and in a way, it's like a legal document. It outlines the requirements for making a certain grade, and it makes clear the penalties for absences, cheating, etc.

In most cases, the syllabus is sacrosanct in a classroom and professors are all too glad to abide by it. Under most circumstances, the syllabus should reign supreme, especially the requirements for various grades. It is OK for a professor to make adjustments to the syllabus during the semester if necessary, as long as everybody is told clearly of the changes.

A change to a syllabus might be necessary for something such as the class not finishing material which might cause a professor to eliminate an assignment or exam, or a professor might give extra credit for something.

91. Most professors would never arbitrarily change a syllabus, but it *can* happen.

I had a situation where my professor was seriously injured in an automobile accident midway through the semester. Another professor assumed responsibility for the class and used a teaching assistant to actually teach the class, though he graded the exams himself.

He changed the terms of the syllabus and I ended up making a B+ in the course when I would have gotten an A under the original syllabus.

I immediately filed a complaint with the undergraduate dean's office. In accordance with the handbook rules, I put the situation and my position in writing, then I met with a representative and argued my case, not unlike a court case.

The professor was given a chance to respond, but I won. The undergraduate dean's office decided in my favor and my B+ was changed to an A, which raised my GPA for that course from 3.7 to 4.0.

Everything counts when you are trying to graduate magna cum laude.

The professor was resentful and he and another professor snubbed me, from then on, when they saw me.

It didn't matter. I won. He lost.

By choice, I would definitely not take courses under either of them in the future.

III
Class

Write fast, but write down everything that comes out of a professor's mouth. That's what I did at the College of Charleston. It is invaluable to have notes like that when test time rolls around. You have a lot of options for producing homemade study guides from a good set of notes, and at the very least, you will be able to go through your notebook and highlight the most important things, tag pages, etc.

92. You must attend EVERY single class.

Even if you are tired, sick, hungover or running late, you MUST go to class. EVERY CLASS.

Don't think it is OK to skip one. It isn't. The one you skip will cover material you will be tested on and you might miss a question because of having missed that one class.

That question might make the difference in an "A" on a test, and a B+. A person who is determined to graduate magna cum laude, or with other honors, should never, ever miss a class.

Period.

I just can't stress this enough. Don't miss class ever.

93. Class is so important that a student can almost pass in college by just going to class.

Almost.

So, when things stack up and you can't get everything done, make sure class isn't the thing you leave out. Go to class.

94. If there is an earthquake, or you are run over by a bus and have to miss a class, make SURE you get good notes from somebody.

Borrow the notebook of a good student and make copies of his or her notes from the class you missed. Tell the student you will be glad to let him/her borrow your notebook if he/she misses a class.

Talk to your professor and make sure you know what was covered the day you missed.

95. You MUST show up for class on time.

Actually, one should be there a few minutes early to settle in, pull out a notebook and get ready to start taking notes.

It is inexcusable to show up late on a regular basis for a class, and professors hate it. So do bosses, friends, and everybody else. It is a disruption for a professor. When class is supposed to start, it is suppose to start right then. Not later. People who show up late for class look slack, like they are so stupid they can't figure out how to get some place on time. Who would want to hire that person!

Now, DO go to class under ALL circumstances. Never skip a class because you are running late, no matter what the reason. It is absolutely critical to go to every single class. If you are late, just apologize to the professor on the way in, apologize again after class, and don't do it again.

96. If you have to brave the elements to get to class, you score big points with your professor, even if you are late.

The rougher and more life-threatening the elements you had to face, the more points you will score.

Downtown Charleston is prone to flooding and I was rushing to class in a torrential rain one morning during a high spring tide down my usual Beaufain Street route when my car was swamped and cut off. I had pulled over before even getting to Colonial Lake, some four or five blocks from the College of Charleston campus.

Got out with umbrella and my back pack and

walked through three feet of swirling water in places, dodging trash cans and other debris floating by. I ended up 30 minutes late and soaked to the bone but that professor loved me even more the rest of the semester.

When you make this kind of effort to get to a class, your professor really appreciates it and you end up the winner.

97. Give your professor the benefit of the doubt if he/she is late to class.

Most of the time, students are required to wait 15 minutes before leaving a class if the professor has not shown up. Most of the time, a late professor will call and somebody from the department will go to the class and let the students know the professor is running late.

But not all the time.

One time, a student pulled a prank on a professor on a test night. We all showed up to find a hand-written note on the door that said the test had been postponed and class canceled. Most students left, but a few of us didn't trust that note and stayed.

The note turned out to be a hoax, probably by somebody who was not prepared for the test. The professor, who was usually prompt, had gotten caught in traffic and was about 10 minutes late for the first time all semester.

When that professor got there to find most of the class gone, he was so thankful for the few who remained that he gave us the test along with easy grading and extra credit for having stayed.

All those who left had to take the test later, which was a pain in the tail for the professor, and he was strict in grading those tests, knowing one of those students was dishonest and had disrupted his class.

98. Observe a respectful and considerate protocol in class.

No sniffing if you can help it. Take medicine to dry your sinuses if you are sick.

No snorting snot up your nose. It is disgusting and distracting.

Don't type, talk, eat, crunch food or paper, or drink water. Sit there and listen, take notes and participate. Be respectful toward the professor and don't disrupt other students.

99. Don't be seduced into just listening to a class lecture and thinking you'll remember it all later. You WON'T.

You absolutely won't. You must actively pay attention and take notes, the more the better.

100. Use pens or pencils for note-taking, whatever you delight in using.

One should use their favorite writing instrument for note-taking. I like #2 pencils because they feel great and write dark, and I can erase if I need to.

I like to buy round pencils that look good and appeal to me aesthetically. This might seem silly but it's not. You need to take a lot of notes, so find an instrument you love and use it.

You might like mechanical pencils. If so, stock up on them.

101. A videotape case is the *perfect* size and structure for pencils, pens, erasers, paper clips, a couple packs of Post-it® Notes, highlighter, etc.

One can easily put over 20 sharpened pencils in a videotape case along with several pens and other supplies such as paper clips, paper clamps, etc.

Definitely include a big eraser for pencils, and an ink eraser.

102. Always put sharpened pencils in your case with the points up.

Then, after you have been writing a while and a pencil's point is dull, you can put it back in the case with the point down (eraser up).

That way you will always know which pencils are sharp and which are dull.

103. Post-it Notes or Sticky Notes® or a generic product are important. So is a highlighter.

I'm taking about a paper product and not any kind of computer software or app. Computer software such as Virtual Notes, that comes as downloadable software or an app, might be fine, but here I'm talking little colored sheets of paper that peel off of a cube or rectangle and will stick to most surfaces, especially other paper surfaces.

The best-known are Post-it® Notes, but Staples, Wal-Mart, Office Depot and others have generic light-tack re-adhesive notes that look the same and are just as good.

Keep a pad of larger and smaller sticky notes in your supply case.

Often the larger notes come in handy if something occurs to you that will help you in another course. Write on the note and tag the other course's notebook with it.

104. There will be times in class when you need to mark passages in a book and Post-it or similar sticky notes will save you a *ton* of time.

Any specific passage a professor discusses in class is worth noting and you can do so easily by underlining or highlighting THEN tagging the page with a small Post-it® Note. Position it so that it sticks a quarter of an inch beyond the top or side edge of the page.

If you don't do this, come test time, you could be flipping through a couple hundred pages looking for underlined or highlighted passages. If pages are tagged, you can go right to them.

If you don't have sticky notes with you, then bend a page's corner down. Do *something* to note a page on which is an important passage.

105. Write down every word a professor says, if possible.

Write fast, but write down everything that comes out of a professor's mouth. That's what I did at the College of Charleston. It is invaluable to have notes like that when test time rolls around. You have a lot of options for producing homemade study guides from a good set of notes, and at the very least, you will be able to go through your notebook and highlight the most important things, tag pages, etc.

Writing things down helps one learn, memorize and retain material anyway.

Write as legibly as possible so you don't have to decipher your chicken scratch later.

If you can't write down every single word a professor utters, then make sure you get ALL of the main points of anything being discussed. It's *all* important because anything can find its way onto a test.

All students should do this, even those not shooting for honors, because the higher the GPA a student ends up with, the better. A good GPA looks better on a job resume and in discussions with potential employers.

106. Tag anything in a textbook or novel or anywhere else that a professor tells you might be on a test.

When a professor tells the class he/she is going over passages or sidebars that will be on a test, reach into your school supply case and whip out your small pad of sticky notes and TAG each page as the professor goes through the book. This is the *best* way to have at your disposal all the things that might be on a test so you can get to studying quickly and not waste time going through the text to locate the passages the professor went over in class.

Also, mark the exact passage with brackets at the beginning and end. Use a highlighter, pencil or pen if you want. Underline or highlight within the marked brackets if need be.

You will have to go fast as the professor goes from one passage to another, but it will be well worth it at study time to have each passage marked and tagged, and you can do it if you have a good school supply case with sticky notes at your disposal that you can pull out quickly.

107. ESPECIALLY note when a professor says that something is the "most important" or "most controversial" or "most" anything.

It's almost certain that passage will be on the test.

108. Write in the margins of books and tag the pages with sticky notes.

There is no substitute for making a comment right next to a passage, especially if a professor has just told you something about it. Don't hesitate to underline sentences, put brackets around paragraphs, note full pages or write in the margins. Tag the pages so you know something significant is on them.

This will be invaluable when test time comes along. You will save you a ton of time in locating passages that will be on a test, and their significance.

Do not worry about whether the book store will buy back your books with notes in the margin. Don't sell your books back. The book store only gives you a pittance for them anyway. You are better off keeping all your college books and starting your own personal library. You can refer back to previous texts when doing research for other courses, or later, when working.

Your books are lovers and you should have your way with them, completely.

If you must sell your books back, then write in pencil and erase your notes before going to the bookstore.

109. Sometimes a student under severe time pressure can skip assigned reading material if he/she goes to every class. However, there are NOTABLE exceptions.

It is best, by far, to read everything because you learn from everything you read. But college students are under time pressure constantly, and if there just isn't enough time to read something, and you know the class is lecture-driven and tests are from lectures, then skip the reading as necessary but make SURE you miss no classes. In fact, pay extra attention and make sure your notes are good. You still may pay a price for this.

Really, the only readings you should ever skip are narrative-type assignments such as found in history and literature; and, as stated above, only skip them if you have to and if you know the material will be covered in class.

110. You should NEVER EVER skip any reading or homework in math, sciences and foreign languages – anything for which your knowledge builds as you progress through the semester.

You must do your reading and ESPECIALLY homework for every class in math, sciences and foreign languages. Of course, this includes statistics and any course using numbers and formulas. If you get behind in a course like that, you better catch up fast or you are dead.

To succeed in any math course, you must work lots of problems so that you can master lower level material and keep advancing with your class. If you get the least bit behind, it becomes extremely difficult, if not impossible, to learn the new material, and you'll get further behind. Many of the sciences are the same way. You must catch up and fast, or be prepared for a low or failing grade.

Foreign languages are demanding too, and require mastery of a new vocabulary and pronunciations, new rules of grammar, etc.

If you are trying to graduate magna cum laude and you get so far behind you can't catch up, drop the course and start over next semester rather than getting a grade that lowers your GPA.

111. The best thing to do is not get behind in math, sciences and foreign languages, and that includes statistics, economics, and any discipline that works with numbers and formulas.

Anticipate the demands you are facing every semester, then, from the opening bell, stay on top of your work!

If you do, you'll be fine.

If you don't, you'll be dead.

112. There is a tremendous side benefit to math, sciences and foreign languages: They *sharpen* the mind like nothing else can.

Working lots of math problems makes the mind nimble and increases your capacity to learn, which benefits you in everything you do in school and life.

Embrace the things you have to struggle with the most because they make you sharper, quicker, and more confident.

This goes to the heart of why a liberal arts education is best (the "liberal" in "liberal arts" comes from antiquity and has NOTHING to do with modern political liberals!).

113. It is good to truly master the basics in lower level language courses. Put a lot into it.

You get your basics in 101 and 102 of any

language course. You find out about other sources of help, other good books and aids that you can get and use before going to the next level.

The 200 level courses always brush you up on 101 and 102, at the beginning. They usually cover more interesting, practical and in-depth material. A good foundation is extremely beneficial and will help you get more out of 201 and 202 including a better grade.

114. Latin can help you learn the Romance languages: Spanish, Portuguese, French, Italian, Romanian and more than a dozen others.

The Romance languages are derived from the common man's spoken Latin, which is called Vulgar Latin. The word "vulgar" as used here comes from the Latin noun *vulgus,* which means "the people, the public . . . the rabble, the mob" (see also the Latin word *vulgaris* meaning "common, ordinary, usual").

Thus, Romance languages are languages that developed after the fall of the Roman Empire in places that had been conquered by the Romans.

One time I left a note for a former wife who was raised in Spain, and at the bottom, I wrote, Te amo! (I love you!).

She came home and got excited and said, "I didn't know you knew Spanish!"

I said I didn't. That was Classical Latin.

115. Latin is a valuable language to know.

So many things are based on Latin such as our legal, scientific and medical terms, but also some 60% of English words.

Again, the Romans conquered Britain then after the fall of the Roman Empire, the Angles, Saxons and others invaded Britain. English, from the Angles, is a Germanic language and it, with other barbarian languages, got mixed with Latin, thus we have Latin's huge influence on our English.

One of my Latin professors gave us a great tip based on the knowledge that some 60% of English words have Latin roots. If we are taking a test, he said, and translating Latin into English, and we don't know the meaning of a Latin word, think of that word as an English word then guess the Latin meaning. His excellent logic was that a guess had a 60% chance of getting you some credit for the word, whereas a blank had a 100% chance of no credit!

There is little emphasis on speaking Classical Latin, so one doesn't need to learn to enunciate and converse, and there is much great history that is studied since the Roman Empire conquered much of the world then morphed into the Catholic Church. Until just a few years ago, Catholic Mass was in Latin, and still is at times; and the influence of Latin on the current Mass is undeniable.

The history of the Roman Empire is the history of Europe, and much of Rome's culture and architecture came from Greece, after Rome conquered Ancient Greece, including Greek gods and goddesses. In the pantheons of Greek and Roman gods, there is a Greek name such as Zeus, and a Roman name, Jupiter. There's the Greek goddess of love, Aphrodite, and the Roman goddess of love, Venus. There's Athena and Minerva; there's Poseidon and Neptune; there's Heracles and Hercules; and on and on.

Latin is fascinating and great to know because Western Civilization comes straight from Ancient Greece and Rome.

116. Studying a spoken language is exciting too, and can help you in our global world, especially with business.

The demands of learning a new vocabulary and rules of grammar, and the culture behind the language, are a lot, but it is stimulating and there's lots of help. You can listen to people who speak the language, and use aids outside the classroom.

Your school will have labs in which people focus on speaking, and fun departmental exercises in which a class might go to a bar or somewhere, but can only speak the language they are studying. No English!

If you're studying Spanish, watch Telemundo!

117. Send emails to fellow students using the foreign language you are studying.

This is an invaluable help to both the sender and recipient. This is an easy way to help yourself learn something.

Also, do things such as writing the date of a class lecture in your notebook in the foreign language you are studying. Use the language any time you can in your life. If you're studying Spanish, read the Spanish labels on products as well as the English.

I used to send emails to fellow Latin students in Classical Latin. It was a great exercise.

118. If you're in a literature class and can't read a novel, then get a study guide such as CliffsNotes or SparkNotes or equivalent, if available.

If you are under pressure and running out of time to complete a novel-reading assignment for a class discussion, then you must do the best you can. Buy a study guide, if available, and read it.

It's a good idea to get a study guide anyway, because they have such good essays and analyses of the material, especially on individual characters, chronology of action, plot, setting, etc.

Use the study guide in conjunction with reading the material itself, and, if something comes up that you don't understand in the text, you may be able to refer back to the study guide for clarification and save a lot of time.

You will absolutely have an easier go of it and get more out of it by reading the novel with a study guide at your side. You will unquestionably learn the material more thoroughly and retain it. You will enjoy the process much more and be better prepared for class.

119. If a study guide on a certain novel is not available, find something online.

If you are trying to get a heads-up on a novel for a class discussion, find something online such as some kind of summary or article that will help.

However, DO NOT EVER copy an article or anything else you've found somewhere and turn it in as your own work. That is plagiarism and is a serious violation for which you can be dismissed from school with tainted record.

It is OK to quote from an article you found online, but you MUST property cite the article, author, publication and other relevant information according to the style of citation required by your professor. And make sure the article is credible and worth quoting.

The best thing to do is read the novel, and use

study guides and articles online as supplements; but, if you absolutely can not finish a novel in time for class, then absolutely use anything you can that will help you.

120. Get the classes you want.

Most schools, nowadays, have computer registration systems. If a class you want is filled up, be relentless about checking your registration system to see if somebody has dropped the class you want. A dropped class will result in an instant opening.

I mean, be relentless! Check it before bed. Check it early in the morning. Check it time to time throughout the day.

Check it several times an hour during the times most people are dropping/adding classes, such as mid-morning.

The College of Charleston has an outstanding course registration system and I would imagine most colleges have similar systems. I have literally been looking at a course with no openings one moment, then checked back seconds later and found an opening. Of course I would jump furiously on it and feel great about it!

Learn your registration system well. Write down course call numbers and check them frequently, or check in the most efficient manner for you.

Usually freshmen and sophomores have the lowest priority when it comes to registration but you can still get a good schedule if you are determined and start the first moment registration opens up for you.

121. When scheduling classes, sometimes it is good to have time in between classes.

Every semester is different but sometimes having an hour or more between classes is invaluable. One can rush to finish a homework assignment, read to prepare for the class, or study for a test. Often a professor will give a 10% participation grade for homework or something else a student can do between classes. There is no excuse for not getting that 10%.

If one can at least read the first few pages of an assignment, he/she can answer the first question or two from a professor and get their class participation grade for the day.

122. Consider longer classes that meet only once a week.

I love longer classes, the kind that meet once a week for two-and-a-half hours. Rather than having to go two and three times a week to a class, you go only once. You then have the freedom to study and do research for a once-a-week class the rest of the week.

Also, students are usually given longer for tests. Even if the tests are longer, having the extra time in a relaxed atmosphere, is nice.

123. Give yourself as many ways as possible to get in a course you want or need. Stack the odds in your favor.

Be aware of every section of a desired course that is offered. Figure out a way that you can accommodate any of those sections that come open.

Maybe one of your other courses has a lot of open sections at different times so you could drop it and grab the desired course if a section came open.

If you are watching three sections of the desired course, you have three times as many chances to get the desired course than if you are only looking at one section. The odds are in your favor.

Think creatively and don't give up until the last minute.

124. Pay special attention during Drop/Add Week, especially the beginning of Drop/Add Week.

If you can get a desired course early in the week, you can attend from the beginning and not miss any classes. Be relentless! Getting in a course that is full isn't going to just happen but it sure as heck can happen.

125. One last resort is a Class Override by the professor.

Many schools frown on these but you might as well try. Often it is up to the professor, and, while there are a lot of rigid go-by-the-rules professors, many are not and will go out of their way to get you in their class.

IV
Grades

The actual quotation belongs to Confucius:
"Choose a job you love, and you will never
have to work a day in your life." **This is the**
foundation of all happiness and success. *If*
you do what you love, you will be so
stimulated by what you do, it won't seem like
work. It will bc fun! So, pursue with all your
heart, your dreams and goals and the things
that stimulate you! Have success, achieve
some great things, make money, find a
partner who makes you happy and live a
great life!

**126. Take advantage of ALL opportunities to
boost your grade by class participation.**

Many professors will base up to 10% of a final
grade on your participation in a class. ALWAYS
get the full percentage by participating. If you are
going to stare at the floor all semester when your
professor asks a question, you are going to lose
10% of your grade in a lot of classes. That is
ridiculous.

Even if your professor does not give a

participation grade, answering questions will help your professor know you, and know you are conscientious. It will definitely translate into a better grade.

127. MAKE yourself answer some short-answer questions in class.

Even if you are shy, hold your breath and shoot up your hand the moment you know an answer, then say the one or two words or the sentence that will answer the professor's question. Be confident. Believe in yourself. Discover your strengths. Overcome your weaknesses.

128. Don't wait to answer a question. You'll get nervous. Do it quickly!

If you wait, you might chicken out.
Don't chicken out.
Look for opportunities to answer questions at the beginning of class.
Pretend like class is JEOPARDY and your professor is Alex or Alexis Trebek. The moment you hear the question, shoot up your hand and say the word or two necessary to answer it, and score!
If you do this enough, your confidence will grow and soon you'll be taking public speaking and making speeches. You'll be looking for opportunities to speak. That's how it works.

129. The better you know your assignment, the more you'll *want* to answer questions.

And you'll feel guilty when you know an answer but are too cowardly like a bck bck bck buuuuckkkkk chicken to answer the question!

Don't be a chicken.

People NEVER sound as bad as they think they do. If you can repeat one or two words, or a sentence, you can answer most questions in a college classroom, and it will definitely get easier the more you do, and it will definitely get you a better grade.

130. If you are shy, you are not alone. A lot of people are petrified of speaking in front of other people.

Don't be one of them. I was once very shy in class myself, and, like the poster says, "I've been rich and I've been poor. Rich is better." – I can tell you that I've been shy and I've been confident. Confident is better.

Work on it because it is important. Don't walk around scared to be asked a question or constantly looking at the floor when the professor asks something.

Put yourself on the path to overcoming shyness. Start by making yourself answer short questions in class.

Join Toastmasters International, which helps

you learn to speak in public. Take a public speaking class at your college. You will be so proud of yourself and it will help you enormously in school and life.

Sit up straight like your mother told you. Answer at least one short question every class. Overcome your fear and get your 10% participation grade.

131. Most participation grades are in smaller classes and not lecture halls.

It is easier to speak out in a small classroom of 20 to 30 students. However, if you find yourself in a larger lecture hall and there is a participation grade, then sit up close, on the first or second row, where you will feel more confident, and apply the "answer the first question you can" method.

If you are more comfortable sitting in the back of a big lecture hall, then do that. Do whatever will work for you, but DO it. Don't chicken out.

132. If you haven't read the assignment, use this trick to get your participation grade.

Read as much as you can of the assignment, at least the first couple pages. Lay low and wait for the first question out of the professor's mouth then shoot your hand up and answer that question before anybody else, because it will likely be the only one you know!

You will appear to be prepared and anxious. Then, for the rest of the period, when a question is asked, you can stare at the floor with the rest of the deadbeats, but *you* will have gotten your participation grade for the day.

I have used this method many times and it works.

133. Potential love interests will think you are bold and confident.

When you answer questions in class, people notice and have a higher opinion of you. Confidence and intelligence are sexy, even if all you did was answer a one-word question at the beginning of every class. That just goes to show how intelligent you really are. You'll get your 10% and be more appealing to love interests at the same time, all because you answered one short question at the beginning of every class.

Of course, if you do one, you can do two or three, and that will add to your aura even more (I'm being facetious but intelligence IS sexy!).

134. Do all the things that will give you 10% here and there because they add up.

For example, if you get credit for posting something each week to a class listserv, by all means do it. Write the page or answer the question or whatever you need to do. Just do the

best you can and turn *something* in, even if you
are pressed for time.

Get in the habit of doing this. Never miss one.
They are easy to do and fast, and they add up.

135. Always do extra credit assignments.

Extra credit assignments are freebies and
make a student look good to the professor. If given
the chance to attend a lecture, play, movie or
other event for extra credit, DO it. Never miss a
chance for extra credit.

136. Ask your professor for extra credit.

If none is offered by the professor, it does not
hurt to ask. He/she might be glad to give you
something extra that will help you.

Suggest something, yourself, to the professor.
Suggest something that you are really interested
in. That is a smart thing to do because you end up
doing something fun and stimulating while
boosting your grade. Always do things like this.

137. Always go for "+"s because they make a huge difference in a Grade Point Average (GPA).

In most grading systems, a student who earns
a B+ in a course will have a higher GPA than a
student who earns only a B.

The reason is the way the GPA is calculated.

GPAs are calculated by multiplying a factor that is determined by the grade the student earns in a course, times the number of credit hours for that course. Here are the grade multiplication factors at the College of Charleston as listed in the *2012-2013 Undergraduate Catalog*:

A   Superior 4.00
A– 3.70
B+ Very Good 3.30
B   Good 3.00
B– 2.70
C+ Fair 2.30
C   Acceptable 2.00
C– 1.70
D+ 1.30
D   Barely Acceptable, Passing 1.00
D– 0.70
F   Failure 0.00

Here is a simple example for a student who has earned a B in a 3-hour course (in a semester system, most courses that meet MWF for 50 minutes are 3-hour (a/k/a 3-credit) courses). The grade multiplication factor for earning a B is 3.00, thus a student's GPA for earning a B in a 3-hour course is 3.00 x 3-hours = 9, which is then divided by the number of hours attempted – in this case 3 – thus the student's GPA would be 9/3 = 3.00.

HOWEVER, a student who earns a B+ uses

the grade multiplication factor of 3.30, therefore
his/her GPA would be calculated by multiplying
3.30 x 3-hours = 9.9, which is then divided by the
number of hours attempted – again, in this case, 3
– thus the B+ student's GPA would be 9.9/3 =
3.30.

The 3.30 GPA is obviously higher than 3.00,
and the student who achieves more pluses in
his/her college career will have a far higher GPA.

It makes a HUGE different when going for
honors, but it also makes a huge difference when
just trying to graduate.

To graduate, a student must have a minimum
GPA and if that minimum is 2.00, then a student
with 1.99 can not graduate. He/she must have a
2.00, and a "+" in a course here and there will
help enormously.

138. Develop a grade STRATEGY based on your situation.

If you are trying to graduate magna cum
laude or with other honors, you don't have to
think too hard to know what you need. You need
straight "A"s, or as close as you can come to them.

Think hard about your unique situation and
be smart. If you are pledging a fraternity or
sorority, playing a sport, working, acting in a play
or have any big demand on your time,
BE SMART.

Rise to the occasion. Pay attention in class. Concentrate harder than if you had less demands on you.

139. Make your study time extremely productive.

Turn off the TV and music. Go where it's quiet like the library and get to work. Work intensely, and focused, then end your study session and go do whatever you need to do.

Use your calendar and KNOW what you have coming up. Look for blocks of time to study, especially if you have regular blocks of time each week.

You will simply have to be more intense about everything and have more desire to achieve if you have big outside demands on your time.

You can do it. In fact, you might end up really excelling because there is a principle at work exemplified by this axiom: If you want something done, ask the busy person. The other kind has no time.

A person used to achieving, who is organized and motivated, can do anything.

Just be acutely aware that you have big demands on your time, therefore, in everything you do, look for the most efficient, effective way to do it. Know that your semester is not "business as usual," that you can do better than you ever imagined with awareness and focus, and the abilities you gain are permanent. You will have raised yourself to a higher, more powerful intellectual level, and you'll have that increased power at your disposal for every endeavor.

140. Drop a course if you need to lighten your work load.

If you are overwhelmed a particular semester, drop a course if you can. Drop your most expendable course.

Make sure you will still be full-time if you need to be, or part-time, so you have no problems keeping a scholarship or financial aid, or staying in good stead with your school.

In most colleges, 12 hours per semester, or more, is full-time; and one can't usually take over 18 hours without special permission.

Remember, your goal is to graduate magna cum laude, NOT graduate in eight straight semesters. If you can graduate magna cum laude in eight, great. But if you need to take less than five courses some semesters in order to make "A" s, then do it. I did.

And don't doubt yourself or feel bad. There is no asterisk on your diploma that says you took nine, ten, 11 or 12 semesters to graduate.

But there WILL BE a very fine notation on your diploma that says you graduated magna cum laude or with other honors.

141. You learn SO much more when you make "A"s.

You become a more powerful intellectual being when you make "A"s. Not only have you learned more, but that knowledge combines with other knowledge you have in a synergy and you end up with way more than the sum of the things you know well. You end up more prone to judgment and wisdom.

A more powerful intellect with judgment helps you achieve anything in life you want, from business success to wooing a love interest. You will undoubtedly have a greater potential for happiness. You will be more competent and confident, and confidence builds on itself.

142. Making good grades makes you more competitive and mentally tougher.

Your quest for good grades is really an intense competition with yourself. You know you can do it if you stay determined and focused.

You become tougher and smarter, and that will help you with all other things in your life. It will also make you prouder of yourself, and more confident.

143. Make it fun: Compete and bet a friend a beer (or a cola if you are underage) on who scores highest on quizzes and tests.

In almost every class I was in, I would become good friends with fellow students and start a betting contest and bet a beer on who would score the highest grade on weekly quizzes, and such. It was a blast. Bet a friend, Megan, in Dr. Phillips' Latin 201 class all semester on translation homework we got back at the beginning of every class. She kicked butt early in the semester but we pulled even toward the end. I ended beating her by five homeworks and she paid off at $1 each = $5 on the day of our final exam! It was great fun all semester and close the whole way. Usually the winner won by just a point or two.

Another good friend and good student, D.J., and I, bet all semester on every test and exam in an upper level history course with nothing but long discussion exercises and exams. The national championship was making the highest grade in the course and we see-sawed back and forth all semester. We were tied going into the final, which I won by one point! Beat him for the semester by *one glorious point* on a final exam! What a great victory! Feel like putting this on my resume!

144. Making "A"s will make you more powerful intellectually than making "B"s; but making "B"s will make you more powerful than making "C"s, all other things being even.

The point is to work as hard as you can to make grades as good as you can because you gain intellectual strength and power in the process.

Of course, if you are wrestling with many difficult things such as holding down a full-time job, raising a family, or playing a sport, these things will also make you stronger, or kill you, as the saying goes.

Don't let them kill you! Don't be beaten! There's no reason for it. You can do anything you truly set your mind to do. Decide that you are NOT going to be beaten, EVER, then develop your plan and get to work.

145. The more active you are mentally, the smarter and more powerful you will become overall.

There is no question about it. If you are active and stimulated by the world and working hard in a lot of different areas, or very intensely in a few or even one, you become stronger, smarter and more powerful intellectually, and that power is there for everything you do in life.

146. The trick is to study what you LOVE, and DO what you love.

I read in the newspaper that the father of the late billionaire Charleston businessman and philanthropist, Jerry Zucker, told him, when he was a young man, something to the effect that "If you do what you love, you'll never work a day in your life!"

The actual quotation belongs to Confucius: "Choose a job you love, and you will never have to work a day in your life."

This is the foundation of all happiness and success. If you do what you love, you will be so stimulated by what you do, it won't seem like work. It will be fun!

So, pursue with all your heart, your dreams and goals and the things that stimulate you! Have success, achieve some great things, make money, find a partner who makes you happy and live a great life!

Teach your children the same attitude. This is America and all things are possible.

147. If you need a certain GPA to maintain a scholarship, then focus on it.

Give it some thought. Develop a strategy. Drop a course if you need to. Go to summer school. Just make sure you are taking enough hours to keep your school and financial aid department happy.

Think about your GPA itself. If you have to have a 3.0 your last semester to graduate, you can do that with two "B"s OR an A and a C OR a B– and B+, etc. Think about everything, then map out a strategy that will work, then do it!

148. If you can't drop a course, then be proactive and deal with the load.

Accept the fact that you have extraordinary demands that semester and map out a strategy to deal with it. Be fearless and more determined than ever. You can certainly do what you set you mind to do. Keep you goals front and center. They are worth it, especially graduating with honors.

Once you graduate magna cum laude, nobody can take it from you, and everybody knows the extraordinary sacrifice and determination that went into it. It does mean you graduated "with great praise" and you deserve it!

V
Studying Effectively

Constantly reading, writing, working problems, researching, thinking, struggling with another language's vocabulary, and the other challenges one faces in college, unquestionably increase intellectual capacity. It's no different from training for a physical competition. One works the body hard, running, weightlifting, swimming, bike riding, and as a result, the body gets stronger, faster, healthier, and the individual is happier, more confident, and more powerful. The intellectual rigors of college life increase a student's brainpower, and that increased brainpower is there for everything in the student's life, from sports, to achievement of personal goals, to wooing a love interest. Brainpower is the key to happiness, and the more one has, the better.

149. Examine your desk calendar at least once a week.

Stay on top of EVERYTHING. Know when it's time to start projects or start studying for tests or start researching for papers and presentations.

Know when all tests are coming up and papers are due. There will be times when two tests, a paper and a presentation all come due the same week.

You can handle it if you have looked at your calendar regularly and planned accordingly.

150. Do not study with the TV on or music playing.

The television is a powerful and compelling force that captures your mind like an electromagnet captures iron filings. You arc kidding yourself if you think you can study effectively with the TV on or music playing. In fact, you are an idiot.

You will waste enormous amounts of time studying with the TV on because that part of your conscious mind captured by the TV is the part you need for study. The little bit left over after the TV gets through with you is not worth a pile of beans.

151. One can accomplish more in 15 minutes of quiet than in two hours with the TV blaring or music playing.

It is far better to pour a cup of coffee and study in quiet, totally focused, when you can think hard about what you are studying and actually understand it on a deeper level. The material will "sink in," which will help you remember it..

Then, you can feel confident that you have achieved something for the day, and you will deserve to crack open a beer (if you are legal) and watch TV or listen to music. At this point, the TV or music are a good thing because they allow you to relax and reward yourself after working hard and really achieving something.

152. Plan your study time. Take control of your life.

If you know you must watch *South Park*, *Jon Stewart* and *The Colbert Report*, then make sure you study with the TV off before they come on, then put down your studying and knock yourself out.

Use common sense and a little planning and your life will go *much* smoother! You will accomplish what you need to accomplish and be less frustrated, or not frustrated at all.

153. Always opt for absolute control over everything.

Don't spend time when you are ready to study, looking through books and stacks of papers for your syllabus or a handout, or an assignment you need to turn in. KNOW where everything is and go right to it. Don't waste time ever.

154. Always follow assignments EXACTLY as given by a professor.

Don't deviate from an assignment. Take each one literally. Do exactly what a professor wants. There is no sense in doing something brilliant then making a "C" because it wasn't what the professor wanted.

Whether an assignment is on the syllabus, or on a handout, or given in class, follow it word for word. If you have any doubt, go talk to the professor and get it cleared up.

155. The key to good grades is figuring out how to teach yourself material fast and effectively, beyond the usual memory tricks.

It's all in the approach. Successful students have taught themselves how to learn and retain material. Others waste time and flounder.

There are numerous effective ways to teach yourself the material you need to know to make "A"s on tests. They usually require more work than average, but not that much more. It's more important to be smart and aware than just put in hours.

156. Create personal study aids for EVERYTHING!

The key to good grades is helping yourself

learn the material fast and effectively. Be creative and determined! Think outside the box!

Once you get in the habit of doing this kind of thing, there is no stopping you, and you are off to a brilliant academic career (or, if you are close to not having the GPA to graduate, it will save your butt and get you where you need to be!)!

157. Keep your eyes open for any kind of study guide that will help you.

For $1, I found a fabulous little guide at the College of Charleston Bookstore for writing literature papers. A professor had created it for the same reason Professor Strunk created the original *The Elements of Style* in 1920—as a guide for his students.

I can not begin to tell you how helpful this little guide was, and still is.

Always look for things like this, that will help you in any of your courses.

158. Make copies of all articles in periodicals, as well as anything your professor has placed on reserve in the library.

You need to be able to write in margins, underline, highlight and tag pages in articles from scholarly publications, and in outside reading, just as with your regular text books. The ONLY way to do it is by making a copy of the article or section of the book.

Be sure and note the publication, volume number, date, page number and any other information necessary for citation.

The best thing to do for citation is include, with the copy of the article or book section, a copy of the title page of said work, and the page with the publisher and copyright information. Staple or paper clip them all together, then you've got everything you need.

159. Always read the footnotes or endnotes in a scholarly article or book. Make a copy of endnotes.

There is good information in footnotes/endnotes. It will help you learn and/or remember material.

It is a pain in the butt to flip to the end of a book or article to read the notes so make a copy of the endnotes and keep it next to you when you read. You'll save a lot of time and make the experience much more pleasurable.

You may find additional sources for papers in footnotes/endnotes.

160. Don't be cheap about copies.

Make copies of any and everything you might possibly need. It's better to have something and not need it, than need something and not have it.

Get in the habit of making copies of all outside research and putting them with your text. When test time rolls around, or papers are due, you will be glad you did.

161. Always buy extra things that will help you.

I purchased a couple different star charts for different courses and they were invaluable. They are nice things to have as part of my personal library.

If a professor suggests something that will be helpful, and you agree, buy it.

162. Buy additional books if they will help you in a course, especially a foreign language.

I bought a copy of *Wheelock's Latin*, by Frederic M. Wheelock, because I had heard from a professor that it was an outstanding Classical Latin text. I was not disappointed. It is an outstanding book. I used it along with my assigned texts. The examples in the back of *Wheelock's Latin* were different from the ones in my assigned texts, as was the glossary. Material was approached differently, which gave me a fresh perspective. Also, there were additional examples and exercises to work.

It was a very smart move. If you know of an additional book or other work that will help you in any course, buy it.

163. There is an unlimited supply of helpful things on the Internet, but be careful.

Of course, make sure you NEVER plagiarize a work found on the Internet. It is dishonest and a dumb thing to do because you can be caught these days and expelled from school, or punished, and you would deserve it.

When using something on the Internet, make sure the source is credible, and properly cite the source, if necessary.

If you are using a study guide from somewhere, make sure it is a good one and is accurate. Remember what your mother told you about copying somebody else's paper. That person might be wrong, thus you would be too! The same applies here.

Check out multiple sources but make sure something you like is absolutely accurate and OK to use, then have at it.

164. Keep valuable handouts on foreign language grammar in a single file folder and close at hand.

This is another simple but EXTREMELY important thing to do. Every time your professor gives you a handout with examples of a particular grammatical construct, put it in a special file folder. Accumulate handouts so they can be accessed quickly when studying.

165. Turn a file folder into a pouch for all your handouts by stapling the sides.

I used to turn each file folder into a pouch by putting five staples a quarter inch from the edges along both sides, so nothing would fall out.

Be creative about study aids and do what will help you cut right to the chase and get to work learning material.

Also, you can imagine how much better off you are when preparing for tests and exam. You have an arsenal of powerful material at your fingertips.

You can take this approach with a lot of courses.

166. Make POWERFUL study aids by making a copy of the help sections in the back of some books so you have them at your fingertips.

I made copies of the glossary in the back of my main Latin text every semester so I could look things up quickly without having to go, awkwardly, to the back of the book. Usually the glossary totaled 10 or 15 pages which was no problem to copy and staple. In fact, I made copies of both the Latin-English glossary AND the English-Latin glossary. I can't begin to tell you how much time one saves by doing things like this.

I also made a copy and stapled the pages together of the grammatical examples in the back of the book. All the basics are there, and having it at my fingertips when translating beat the hell out of flipping to the back of the book, then flipping back to the passage.

I was able to look at both the passage I was translating AND the grammar help from the back of the book at the same time. This was extremely helpful.

The goal is to learn material and not waste time looking for things.

167. My Latin file folder of grammar handouts and aids was awesome and actually made translating fun.

In addition to the stapled copies of the glossary, and stapled copies of all the grammatical constructs from the back of my main text book *and* the back of Wheelock's Latin, I had a legal-size sheet with the five declensions and their endings as well as all the cases and examples of all the possible usages, homework assignments that were particularly good examples of things like indirect statements, lots of indicative and subjunctive verb synopses from my custom-made fill-in-the-blank sheets, pages and pages of vocabulary including a word and all its endings which are numerous in Latin, a handout on "purpose" and "result clauses," handout on present indicative and subjunctive endings with the trick, "We beat a liar," handout on noun declension endings, handout on conjugating with the present stem, handout on conjugating perfect tenses, active and passive, test review guides, several handouts on participles and infinitives, a handout on indirect statements, a handout on infinitives and indirect statements, and more.

These things saved me tons of time and enabled me to wrestle with the material and not look in frustration for a handout on something.

Always dedicate and label specific file folders for valuable handouts and accumulate the handouts in one place - the labeled file folder - throughout the semester.

Always do these kinds of things in every course.

168. When translating a foreign language passage for homework, create practice sheets that break the passage apart sentence by sentence *(see illustration below)*.

At the top of a blank page, type the first sentence using 14 point type and leaving an *inch* of space between lines, and *three* inches between sentences. This will give you plenty of room to work. You'll only have two or three sentences per page.

Print it, then make multiple copies of each sheet (or print multiple copies) so you can practice until you are perfect. Keep some copies for final exam preparation.

Having plenty of room to translate each individual sentence is extremely valuable. When you go over them in class, you can scratch and write corrections, make comments about grammatical constructs, etc.

Later in the semester, perhaps in studying for your final exam, you will have the corrected sheets you used in class as your guide.

You can then pull out some fresh practice sheets and re-translate the sentences. This will be excellent preparation for your final. Your guide will be the sheet you used in class on which is written complete grammatical information on each sentence from your class discussion, and each sentence will be translated perfectly. You will be set!

Lesson XXXVII

Civil War

[M. Tullio Cicerone oratore et C. Antonio consulibus,] (Ablative absolute expressing time: *in the consulship of* (63 B.C.). The Romans used the names of the consuls to date the year.) L. Sergius Catilina, vir nobilissimi generis, ad delendam patriam coniuravit cum quibusdam claris quidem, sed audacibus viris.

With the orator Marcus Tullius Cicerone and in the consulship of

Claudius Antonio, Lucius Sergius Catilina, a man of most noble birth,

he swore together toward destroying the country with a certain, with certain men... were indeed daring, but with daring men.

A Cicerone urbe expulsus est. Socii eius comprehensi occisi sunt.

He was driven out from the city by Cicerone. His allies having been seized were killed.

Catilina ipse victus proelio est et interfectus.

Catilina himself was conquered in battle and killed.

Homemade sheets that give you plenty of room to translate foreign language passages then correct them in class, are invaluable. The corrected sheets will be extremely helpful when preparing for your final exam. The above sample was originally letter size (8-1/2 x 11").

169. ALWAYS DO ALL HOMEWORK in math, sciences, foreign languages, statistics, economics - any course that uses numbers and formulas or for which knowledge builds as you progress through the semester.

For math, sciences, foreign languages, etc., you have GOT to do your homework and work lots of problems and translate lots of passages, then go to class and get the right answers when the professor goes over homework. To have problems worked with all the right steps and the correct answers, and accurate translations of foreign language passages, are INVALUABLE when test time rolls around.

Most of these kinds of courses are cumulative. It is a GREAT help to have perfectly corrected homework featuring problems you haven't looked at in weeks, that will be on your final exam.

170. You can "Google" anything these days, so do it. It enhances study and research.

You can make Google your default search engine for any browser.

Or, you can put a little Google toolbar on your browser. You can download one from Google free.

If you are working on a paper or doing any kind of writing and get stumped, simply Google the thing you are stumped about. Something will pop up!

Make SURE it is the thing you are looking for. Usually Wikipedia pops up first. Check Wikipedia against other credible sites such as a good university website, or Encyclopedia Britannica Online.

If you need to cite something, make sure you get the information you will need for proper citation.

171. If you can't think of a term or title, Google what you know.

For example, recently I couldn't think of the name of Edgar Allan Poe's essay, "The Philosophy of Composition." I kept thinking "Art of Composition." It was driving me crazy so I did a quick Google search with terms "Poe composition" and the correct name instantly appeared on a number of web sites: "The Philosophy of Composition."

I felt relieved.

172. Do outside things to help learn an assignment.

If you have to read a Shakespeare play, then go to the library and check-out a DVD of a performance of that play. The BBC produced many of Shakespeare's plays that include some of the finest Shakespearean actors on earth, and they are exactly true to the script. One can read a script along with the action on the screen to get an interpretation of any scene.

This is a fun thing to do and greatly enhances your experience as well as helps you learn and remember.

Do this kind of thing with everything you are studying. If you are studying something in a class, and a lecturer comes to town to lecture on that subject, go see him/her. If a movie comes out, or one already exists on DVD of a subject you are studying, go get it.

Always be thinking this way.

173. When reading plays, go see a performance of said play.

It is exciting and eye-opening to read a play for a class assignment then go see a performance of that play. Of course, play scripts and interpretations are often changed by directors and producers so make sure you know the details of the performance.

I've seen *Lysistrata* many times and it has been produced with new twists quite often, but each performance still has the theme of women, tired of war between Athens and Sparta, humorously withholding sex from their husbands in order to force a rapid close to the war.

The last performance I saw was at the College of Charleston and the characters were more modern (for example, the Spartans were cowboys), BUT there were enlarged erect penises on the male characters to demonstrate the power of the women to effect the men's behavior.

And those props were historical and accurate because the Ancient Greeks often used enlarged phallic symbols on men, and enlarged breasts on women, on the stage to make their points!

Go out of town if you have to, but see a performance of any play or literary work you are studying. Have fun. Get a date. Make a weekend of it.

174. Look at DVDs on people you are studying, especially literary people whose works you are studying.

Short biopics are interesting and helpful, especially on authors whose works you are studying. It enriches your experience greatly to understand the author and his/her times. It's enjoyable to kick back and watch something, and it's good to be able to rewind and look at certain parts several times.

A student increases his/her frame of reference about a work or author by adding knowledge about the work or author beyond the class assignment. Always do things like this because, not only are they enjoyable, they are easy and fast ways to gain additional knowledge, and they help you retain what you've learned.

175. When reading a novel, taking notes helps enormously.

Use a separate pad, notebook or the last 30 pages of your current notebook. If you use the last 30 pages of your current notebook, then tag the top of the page on which you begin. You can let a quarter of an inch of the tag stick up above the page, then write on that quarter of an inch the title of the novel or a keyword from the title so you can go right to it.

176. Always put the novel's page number by *each* of your notes.

Then later, when you are writing your paper or preparing your presentation, or if you need to clarify a point for a test, you can go right to the page in the novel that your note refers to.

Don't hesitate to make notes on anything that will be of value in your analysis. It makes class discussions, papers and presentations go so much better.

177. In your notes, jot down the main things as you encounter them in a novel.

The main things that will help you understand a novel as you go along are character names and relationships, place names, dates, character ages, and any important action. Taking a few notes will make the book much more clear to you from the beginning and more enjoyable. You'll get more out of it.

Jot down anything else that occurs to you. You might end up writing a compare/contrast paper and if something occurs to you from another work, write it down so you don't lose the thought.

178. Always write your thoughts down as you read. If you don't, you'll lose most of them.

When you encounter a character, pages later, who is the daughter of the main character, then flip to the main character's name and under it write the daughter's name and her page number. Later, when she has a baby, go back to the daughter's name and write the baby's name, birth date, and anything else important.

This is the kind of thing to do with a novel, and it will make it much more clear and pleasurable, and you will understand it better.

179. A trick to use if crunched for time with a novel.

Carefully read the first 50 to 100 pages, skim FAST the middle section, then carefully read the last 50 to 100 pages. This method helps because the early careful reading gets one into the novel, and the later careful reading brings one to the denouement.

Of course, novels ought to be read and savored, every single word of them, especially famous works of art in the literary canon. There is a reason they are in the literary canon! A student is cheating himself/herself by not poring over these works and enjoying them thoroughly.

It is true that fiction often demonstrates the truth of the human situation better than non-fiction—better than truth itself. There is much to be gained by knowing and pondering the knowledge of humanity in the world's great literature.

But day-to-day living and college life are often demanding and don't leave time to get everything done. When that happens, use every trick at your disposal to get as much out of an assignment as you can, especially if it affects your grade.

180. CliffsNotes, SparkNotes and similar study guides are helpful.

Even when one has the time to read a novel carefully, CliffsNotes, SparkNotes or similar study guides help because they list characters and details, and often have critical essays on the work.

Try never to substitute CliffsNotes or SparkNotes for reading the work itself, but if there is simply no time because you have tests and papers due and a working life, then, by all means, read a study guide and don't feel guilty.

181. A movie based on a novel will be somewhat different from the novel, and that's OK.

A movie screenplay based on a novel is a different art form from the novel that inspired it. Usually the basic theme of the book, at least, is presented in the movie.

It is not a commentary on the movie, good or bad, whether it is more true to the novel or less. They are two separate works of art, and art forms.

However, it is interesting and irresistible to note how similar a movie is to a book.

I actually think the movie, *Gone with the Wind*, is very true to Margaret Mitchell's novel, though some details, including the famous last line of Rhett Butler, were changed. In the novel, Rhett said, "My dear, I don't give a damn."

In the movie, it is the immortal words, "Frankly, my dear, I don't give a damn."

The addition of "frankly" is fabulously effective in the movie, but not having it in the book takes nothing from the book.

182. Intense school work sharpens the mind.

Nothing makes a person intellectually sharper and quicker than reading, researching, writing papers, doing math problems and struggling with the grammatical conventions of a foreign language.

Students will sometime say that they will never have to use art history or a math course so why should they have to take it?

The reason is because a good liberal arts education broadens a student's perspective and knowledge like nothing else can. It exposes the student to major areas of science, economics, history, literature, art and business, just to name a few, and those fields are important.

Exposing a person to a new field might stimulate an interest that can lead to a career or life-long passion. A stimulated, motivated person is just the kind to make important contributions to society.

183. It's not only the knowledge one gains, but abilities and skills are honed.

One has to THINK about things in college, constantly, and arrive at his/her own conclusions. One has to write and argue points. Students have to use discipline in their personal lives to make sure they go to class on time, take good notes, study effectively, turn in papers before deadlines, and make good enough grades on tests and papers to graduate magna cum laude, or at least graduate.

Constantly reading, writing, working problems, researching, thinking, struggling with another language's vocabulary, and the other challenges one faces in college, unquestionably increase intellectual capacity. It's no different from training for a physical competition. One works the body hard, running, weightlifting, swimming, bike riding, and as a result, the body gets stronger, faster, healthier, and the individual is happier, more confident, and more powerful.

The intellectual rigors of college life increase a student's brainpower, and that increased brainpower is there for everything in the student's life, from sports, to achievement of personal goals, to wooing a love interest. Brainpower is the key to happiness, and the more one has, the better.

A liberal arts education increases brainpower like nothing else can.

VI
Preparing for Tests / Exams

Exam Preparation Triage . . . There will be many times when you have several tests, papers or other work all due the same week, especially at mid-term. When that happens, do what military doctors and nurses do after a battle when wounded soldiers are lying around bleeding and drying: analyze the situation and save the largest number you can in the shortest period of time by going to those who can be stabilized quickly, then moving to the more needy.

184. Make sure you go to ALL classes as you get closer to test time.

You should never miss a class anyway! But ESPECIALLY don't miss any of the two or three classes before a test.

Your last class before a test might be the only review the professor gives. If you miss it, definitely call somebody in the class and get their notes with the test prep.

185. The class before a test, a professor will usually go over what will be on the test. This is when sticky notes really help.

The class before a test is usually when a professor will go fast through material in your book that you will need to know.

For example, say you're in a literature class and you've covered 200 pages of stories by different authors. On the test will be passages from various stories. You are expected to know the character or event each passage is about, the work each passage came from and its author, and the passage's significance. I had numerous tests like this at the College of Charleston.

The class before the test, when the professor is flipping at the speed of light through the book telling you that you need to know this passage and that passage, you better be tearing off Post-it Notes like greased lightning and tagging those pages and writing in the margins.

When you are ready to study, those tagged pages will give you a huge heads up. You can get right to studying instead of wasting time looking for highlighted passages in 200 pages of text. On the test, you will *nail* them all.

The same principle applies to most courses. Tag important pages and save yourself a *ton* of time!

If you don't have sticky notes with you, at

least bend the corners of the pages, which might help.

186. Go to EVERY test review and study session.

Most of the time, the material covered by a professor in a test review or study session is exactly what will be on a test. Any problem a professor works, you better believe that type of problem will be on the test.

Take advantage of test reviews and study sessions. You will make a good impression on your professor, who will think you are conscientious and motivated.

187. A videotaped study session is extremely helpful in some courses, especially sciences and math, in which there are problems to solve.

I videotaped a study session for a friend who was sick, one time, and it was invaluable to her. I zoomed-in on the board when problems were written-out, discussed and solved by the professor.

My friend was able to pause, rewind, and listen to things the professor said, over and over, until they sunk in. She was able to master the material and do well on her test.

It was work to videotape that study session, but the professor did not mind in the least, and the tape turned out to be a great tool. It also helped my friend prepare for her final exam weeks later.

If you find yourself in a similar situation, ask your professor if you can videotape a study session then grab your camera and go for it. A tripod is almost a necessity so that the video produced is smooth and not shaky.

188. Do Exam Preparation Triage when you run out of study time.

There will be many times when you have several tests, papers or other work all due the same week, especially at mid-term. When that happens, do what military doctors and nurses do after a battle when wounded soldiers are lying around bleeding and drying: analyze the situation and save the largest number you can in the shortest period of time by going to those who can be stabilized quickly, then moving to the more needy.

The actual definition of "triage," in *The Oxford American College Dictionary*, 2002 edition, is:

> **triage** – n. 1 the action of sorting according to quality. 2 (in medical use) the assignment of degrees of urgency to wounds or illnesses to decide the order of treatment of a large number of patients or casualties. v. (trans.) assign degrees

of urgency to (wounded or ill patients).

Here's the same definition online: http://oxforddictionaries.com/ definition/english/triage.[16]

If you have ever seen episodes of the famous TV series, *MASH*, think about the beginning of any episode when the choppers come flying in fast and low with battle wounded. Everybody is running to the landing field to get to the wounded quickly so they can analyze and start treating all those who can be saved right away, while preparing to work on the more needy cases.

They have to make tough decisions because they can't spend time on someone who needs a lot of care while three others die who could have been saved with a little care. They are out to save as many as they can, out of the chaos.

189. Exam Preparation Triage works like *MASH*.

Analyze according to need. If you have a solid "A" in a course and are well-prepared, pay less attention to it than the course in which you have a B+ that needs to be pulled up to an A. Now, don't

---

[16] Definition of "triage" in Oxford Dictionaries online, accessed March 26, 2013, http://oxforddictionaries.com/ definition/english/triage

EVER let an A slip away. Make sure you cover the A, then move on to more pressing needs fast.

You might have a paper due that can get you an A in a course, and you might want to concentrate on it.

If you are simply trying to graduate, and you know you can not make better than a B in a course, then spend enough time to assure your B, while spending more time pulling a D up to a C.

190. You might have a more complicated need.

You might need to make three "B"s in order to bring a GPA up to 2.0 so you can graduate. If that is the case, then design your triage accordingly. Look at other ways you might meet your goal such as making an A, a B, and a C. It could get you the same GPA as three "B"s and be more achievable. Just analyze the entire situation thoroughly then get to work.

The more effective you are at Exam Preparation Triage, the more successful you will be academically. You will have to think this way many times in college, as well as in life. It's good to be familiar with it now.

191. While crunched for time in the middle of Exam Preparation Triage, plan smartly.

Study the things you know will have the

highest likelihood of being on an exam.

Study the things you know will have the highest point value on the exam. If a professor has given you a study guide, analyze it thoroughly and use it to plan your strategy.

192. There will be times when you need to forget about what you don't know, and study what you know.

If you are way behind in a course, and you know you will not be able to teach yourself some difficult concept the night before a test, then forget about it. Study what you know. Study what you can nail on the test. Guarantee yourself some points.

I'm not talking to students with a chance to graduate magna cum laude because those students would never be way behind the night before a test. I'm talking to students who have been partying too much and procrastinating and now find themselves with much they don't know and no time to learn it.

193. MAKE AN "A" ON EVERY SINGLE TEST, GUARANTEED, with my brilliant Unconventionally-Typeset Printouts *(see illustration below).*

Think outside the box!
I created an EXCELLENT method that almost

always guaranteed me an "A" on a test. It required some work but it was in doing that work that I learned the material because it drove the material deep into my brain.

It starts with good class notes, which is why it is imperative that a student never miss class and always write down every word a professor utters, or at least the gist of every point a professor makes in a lecture. With notes this good, the student can then prepare for a test, two or three days before the test, by first typing into any word processing program everything from the student's notebook that will be on the test.

Then, to emphasize various notes and drive things into one's brain, the student should typeset those notes in sort of an unconventional way by making important words or phrases bold, by increasing the point size of other words, phrases, definitions and the like, by centering other points, by using italics, by using increased-point-size italics, by using a different type style here and there. The point is to make your notes jump off the page!

In the process of doing this, the material will go deep into a students brain.

The student should print those creatively typeset notes and staple the several pages together then have your way with them by underlining in red or tagging pages or using asterisks or any other method the student likes to add even more emphasis to the most important things.

c:\stdyfl98\1st251ex.pm5

1st 251 (Cosmos) exam.:
Thursday, 24 September 1998

Life on earth might be a fluke because we are not part of a binary stellar system and
most other stars are, which causes "wild" gravity which might prevent life from
developing on a binary star.

EAST is most sacred direction (sun rises); WEST next, since sun sets there

Ancients learned the cycle of the **solstices** (Latin for "sun stand still") \
equinoxes (day and night the same)

Humans began Neolithic Revolution/agriculture independent of each other:
- wild grains/seed
- grasses for animals
- animal husbandry (used dogs but earlier had eaten them)
- pastoral husbandry

"Civil" in "civilization" means "city"

Throughout all time, homo sapiens the same in needs

Down to 1000 BC all humans had same relationship wtih universe ("cosmic man")

BIRTH / DEATH / RE-BIRTH

Cosmos: an orderly, harmonious, systematic universe
(**CHAOS** the opposite); order, harmony

Cosmology: a branch of astronomy that deals with the
order of the universe; opposite is *CHAOS;* also, the study
of the structure and evolutoin of the entire universe.

My Unconventionally Typeset Printouts
DRIVE KNOWLEDGE into your brain! Here, I
use oversized text, all caps, and bold type, but
this sheet is mild. You should go crazy with
centering, large italics, different typestyles
and whatever else it takes to cause facts to
JUMP OFF THE PAGE into your brain!

Cosmogony: CREATION OF the order of the universe; also, the creation or origin of the world or universe; **a theory of the origin of the universe**

Illiad and Oddsessy first written myths

Cosmic Man no need for history/linear time, just cyclical time.

lingua franca: any of various languages used as common or commercial tongues among peoples of diverse speech: **the COSMIC language was the lingua franca of the ancients**

9 moon cycles = pregnancy and birth

365 days to go through 4 seasons

Ancient man simply wanted cycles to keep going

Microlith - small stone to fashion tools, weapons, things to worship; big step to

MEGALITHS: Megalithic astronomy: must be before 1800 BC; aligned to astrological events

Only civilization to break out of cyclical existence was Western European which gave rise to us; it behind in 1500 but quickly caught up

NOTED AS "GOOD" EXAM QUESTION: In 1965, Alexander Marchack examined Upper Paleolithic (20,000 to 30,000 years ago) bone markings under a microscope and he photographed them. He discovered the scratches were "not simply decoration " but lunar observations. This give evidence that the oldest known calendars (or markers of the passage of time) were the systematic notations "carved on bones by Ice Age people in the Upper Paleolithci period 20,000 to 30,000 years ago," making it contemporary with great cave art. He specifically examined a bone from the Blanchard rock shelter in France and it encouraged him to intensify his study until he became convinced the bone markings were some kind of lunar calendar or record.

Note my last comment above, which came out of my notebook: NOTED AS "GOOD" EXAM QUESTION. Dr. Reynolds had said in class that this was a good exam question, so you better believe I was ready for it, and it WAS on the exam! This page and the previous one were originally letter size (8-1/2 by 11").

194. A student who gets behind will find my Unconventionally-Typeset Printouts invaluable.

A student in danger of failing a course or worse – not being able to graduate – must pull out all the stops. This kind of student would not usually retype the relevant part of his/her notebook before a test but this is WAR, and whatever a student retypes into their Unconventionally-Typeset Printout will be driven deep into the student's brain. Especially if the student then has his/her way with the printout by underlining the most important things in red, using asterisks, highlighting, tagging sections, etc., etc.

If a student has mediocre notes, then the Unconventionally-Typeset Printout will have less value *but*, that being the case, the student should borrow the notes of a classmate or friend. It is far better to go into a critical test prepared than to sit on one's butt and fail a course or not graduate.

195. If there is no time to type all your notes, then highlight and tag right in your notebook.

Type what you can, but if there is little or no time for typing in notes from your notebook, then go through the notebook itself and underline things in red, use big asterisks, tag pages, highlight and do things that will make important points jump out.

196. Let me reiterate that typing the notes from your notebook is a tremendous way to learn test material easily.

It is incredible how well one learns material that has been typed from a good set of notes in a notebook using different type sizes, bold, italic, bullets, centered paragraphs, etc. The process of typing drives material deep into the brain and it is retained and recalled adeptly for the test, and later if the exam is cumulative.

Also, when studying for a cumulative exam, you can pull out the Unconventionally-Typeset Printout from the midterm and there is everything, jumping off the page and back into your brain!

197. For math, sciences and foreign languages, there is no substitute for working tons of problems.

Of course, going to every class and doing ALL homework is absolutely critical in math, sciences and foreign languages. Staying current with the class is imperative.

A student must know how to work every type math or science problem that will be on a test, and a student must know the grammatical constructs and vocabulary of a foreign language. There is no way around it. A student who has worked lots of problems or translated lots of

sentences will have a piece of cake with tests.
They will actually be fun.

Smart students anticipate tests, days and
weeks ahead of time, and work the requisite
problems and/or translate the requisite material.

198. Create your own practice tests.

This is another GREAT exercise, especially for
math, sciences and foreign languages. When a test
approaches, create your own practice test by
taking problems from old homework assignments,
at the end of chapters, in workbooks and
especially problems the professor has gone over in
class. Write the problems but not the answers, on
blank paper, leaving space beside each problem
for your work, as if it was an actual test.

Make several copies of your blank practice
test then sit down and take your practice test over
and over and over, under simulated test
conditions, until you can work every problem.
When you can, you are ready for your real test
and will likely ace it.

199. You can and should create practice tests for most subjects.

For a foreign language, have vocabulary
words to translate next to blank lines, then fill in
the blanks!

Practice translating passages or declining

nouns or conjugating verbs. Practice, practice, practice, but help yourself do it with practice tests you have created, that have no answers and plenty of blanks to fill in.

Make lots of copies of your practice tests so you can work them until you are perfect.

Insert a passage to translate. Perhaps use two or three or several different passages.

Put each passage on a separate sheet so you can concentrate on just it.

Make lots of copies of your sheets of passages so you can work each of them until you are perfect.

Be creative! Once you've made lots of copies of your blank test and sheets of passages and anything else, then practice, practice, practice by filling them in under simulated test conditions.

200. Create fill-in-the-blank exercises for any subject because they are EXTREMELY helpful.

You can cut to the quick and create exactly what you need. Be creative. Once you have a master with blank lines to fill in, make 50 copies at a time, then work a few every day under simulated test conditions, especially as test time approaches.

These are invaluable exercises and the right way to be thinking, always.

Remember, the key to good grades is knowing

how to teach yourself material quickly and effectively, so you understand it and can retain and recall it on tests.

201. Fill-in-the-blank exercises are especially valuable with foreign languages *(see illustrations below).*

For example, I created Latin verb synopsis sheets that were INVALUABLE. I had one for the Indicative mood and another for Subjunctive.

The Indicative was legal-size and started with blank lines across the very top for the four parts of the Latin verb, and under that was "Indicative." The Subjunctive was letter-size and started the same, with the four parts of the Latin verb across the top and "Subjunctive" under it.

I took my clean masters and made 50 copies at a time and would fill-in the copies constantly.

Do a Google search for synopsis sheets for whatever language you are studying, and, almost assuredly, some good aids will pop up.

Here are mine with the verb "To Be" filled in:

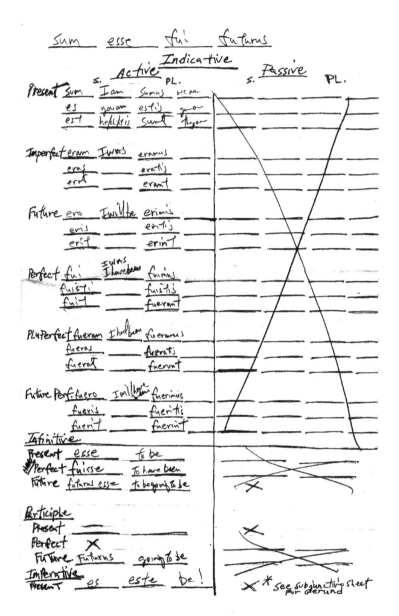

sum   esse   fui   futurus

Indicative

Make 50 copies at a time of your clean masters, and fill them in regularly. This was originally legal size (8-1/2 x 14").

Sum   esse   fui   futurus

subjunctive

Active | Passive

	S.		PL.		S.	PL.

Present: sim letmebe simus let us be
sis let you be situs let you be
sit let him be sint let them be

Imperf. essem ___ essemus
esses ___ essetis
esset ___ essent

Perfect fuerim ___ fuerimus
fueris ___ fueritis
fuerit ___ fuerint

Plюperf. fuissem ___ fuissemus
fuisses ___ fuissetis
fuisset ___ fuissent

Gerund
Gen ___ Dat. ___ Accus. ___ Abl. ___

Nom. is Present Active Infinitive

This was originally letter size (8-1/2 x 11").

202. Here's another good example of a practice test, this one using a star chart.

We had to identify constellations in a Cosmos in History class one time. I took a class handout, whited-out the names of the constellations, then made 25 copies. I'd practice filling in the names of the constellations and when test time rolled around, I nailed that part of the test.

This approach can be used with any number of things and it helps a student learn material fast and effectively. Always be thinking this way!

203. When preparing for a test, remember the "MOSTS."

Anything your professor says is the "most" something, take note, whether it's "most controversial" or "most famous" or "most anthologized." It will likely be on your test.

When reading, note the most *anything*.

Whether reading your book or taking notes in a class, when you come across or hear a "most," use an asterisk, highlighter or underline it, and tag the page. The "mosts" are always important, and MOST of the time they will be on a test.

204. Note everything a professor emphasizes in a lecture.

There's a reason the professor emphasized it.

He/she wants you to know it, even if the emphasis was small.

205. Marijuana is illegal in most places, but if you smoke pot, DON'T smoke anywhere near an important test or exam.

I am not advocating marijuana by any stretch of the imagination, but it is well known that a lot of college students smoke pot, so I am going to address it here – honestly – in order to help college students, which is the purpose of this book.

206. I KNOW how pot works.

Pot dulls your sharp edge, slows your brain and stays with you for days. Some people think that is not the case, but it absolutely is the case.

The best way to take tests is with a clear mind after a good night's sleep, a meal and cup of coffee.

If you've been smoking pot, try to get as much out of your system before a test, as possible. Run, walk, swim, do anything that will raise your heart rate and cause your body to flush out poisons. The fresh air will do you good anyway.

207. Smoking pot when doing research for papers will slow or shut you down. Don't waste your valuable time.

Writing papers requires a sharp mind to

ferret out good sources, and it is imperative that one stay organized and on track. Pot, again, dulls your sharp edge. You don't want to be sitting in the library thinking about something you saw on *The Colbert Report* when you should be pressing forward with research for a paper whose deadline is fast approaching.

208. Most people can not do research while stoned.

Even if you are already organized and simple go to the library, stoned, to check out some books, you still short-change yourself because any book you are looking for, and locate in the stacks, will have lots of others on the same topic around it. It will be a gold mine for your research and if you had a good sharp mind you could go through those other books, too, instead of dying to go get something to eat or listen to music.

Get your work done first, then relax.

209. Don't study when stoned. It is a WASTE of time.

Trying to study when stoned is EXTREMELY inefficient and has only a marginal benefit. Why read the same paragraph five or six times and then not remember what is in it? If you are normal (I mean, *not stoned*), you could read it once and move on.

Also, your ultimate retention, when stoned, is pathetic. You, seriously, will not remember as much about that paragraph if you are stoned when you read it.

Always study first, with a clear mind. You will get your studying done a lot faster and get a lot more out of it.

210. Most "brilliant" ideas one gets when stoned have to be discarded the next day anyway.

You can be sitting there stoned and get a brilliant idea and write it down, admiring your intelligence, then the next morning look at your note and think, "What the hell did I write that for!"

That is what happens most of the time to pot-induced brilliance. It becomes the next morning's joke.

Now, time to time, one might truly get a good idea when stoned, but believe me – and I am speaking from MUCH experience – the pot is not what caused the good idea. Your brain did.

211. Your mind will sharpen from using it in school, but smoking pot when studying for a test is STUPID.

There is no question that people who apply themselves to any intellectual pursuit, sharpen their minds. One can work a lot of math problems and afterward feel sharp as a tack, the opposite of that sleepy, drifting pot-high feeling.

Smoking pot when studying for a test is stupid. It wastes lots of time and reduces your effectiveness in learning material.

Same with research. Pot causes you to waste time.

212. If you have been smoking pot but have an important test approaching, stop smoking and get some exercise to work it out of your system.

The more pot you can get out of your system, the better off you will be on test day. You will also study better before the test.

Do aerobic exercise that gets your heart rate up for 45 minutes or longer, like running, bike riding, walking or swimming; but any exercise is good.

213. Exercising is always a great thing to do.

A fitness program will keep you at your peak. It will make all intellectual pursuits more effective.

When you are out running or walking, you are in the fresh air which stimulates your mind and goes great with your elevated heart rate and metabolism. Think about things you have been studying. Wrestle with problems. Plan papers. Strategize about your life and goals.

214. Another huge benefit of exercise is stress reduction.

Our daily lives give us a certain amount of tension and stress, and to that, college students must add the tension and stress of classes and grades (and pursuing potential love interests).

Exercise reduces stress. It loosens tight muscles. It flushes out your system. It causes you to look better, be stronger, more confident. It causes your body to work better which causes your mind to work better. Exercise, and a happy healthy life, go hand in hand, and a regular exercise program fits nicely with the college lifestyle.

On the other hand, couch potatoes are usually overweight, sluggish, have less energy, don't look as good as they could, and their bodies retain all the poisons put into them longer.

People who exercise can party more with less bad repercussions.

215. Do exercise a lot, and regularly, but don't overdo it the day before a test or even two days before a test.

Being physically broken down from strenuous exercise makes one lethargic and dulls one's edge. Be smart about exercise. Going for an easy run or walk the day before a test, or even the day of a test, is fine.

But don't run 20 miles or ride a bike 50 the day or even two days before a test. If you do, you will be tired physically and mentally on test day.

216. The goal is to be at your PEAK on test day or game day.

I've run four marathons and over 50 other races of varying distances, mostly 10Ks.

The principle of physical conditioning is to workout hard then give your body a chance to recover. It is after the recovery that one emerges stronger and more fit. The better shape you get in, the more you can do, and the stronger you are after recovery.

Runners mix it up with something like this: a long run one day, a short run the next, a hard speed workout the next, an easy run the next, a medium run at race pace, etc., etc.

The point is that you should not do a hard workout every day. Your body must have time to recover and repair itself. Hard/easy, hard/easy, or some variation, is a great way to get in shape.

You want to peak and be at your mental best the day of a test just as you want to peak and be at your physical (and mental) best the day of an athletic event.

If you have been training hard or doing a lot of exercise, then two or three days before your test, start with light workouts. Do easy runs or rides. Maybe walk some. Do nothing that taxes you, so that your body can heal and build itself up to a physical and mental peak when you need it.

217. Get a good night's sleep before a test.

There is no question that you will do better on a test if you get a good night's sleep. Your mind will be sharper and memory better. You will be able to do problems faster and with more confidence.

The worst thing to do is be so far behind you have to pull an all-nighter. If you feel like you must stay up all night to catch up, then fine. I've done plenty of all-nighters myself, but it's best to avoid them if possible, and it is always good to get *some* sleep, even an hour or two. Just make *sure* there is no way you can oversleep.

218. Do not go out for a quick beer with friends the night before a test unless you have IRON discipline.

Too often it is easy to be seduced by the thought of a quick beer with friends who don't have a test the next day, but then that quick beer turns into four or five and first thing you know it is 2:00 a.m. and you have been dancing for three hours and have a 9 a.m. exam.

It is best to be protective of the night before a test. Don't go out unless you know you can limit yourself to one beer and be home early.

The worst thing you can do on test day is have a hangover, or be queasy from drinking too much the night before, or, God forbid, oversleep.

219. Do not encourage friends who have tests the next day to go out with you.

Cut your friends some slack. Be considerate of them. If you know they have a test the next day, tell them to stay home and study and get a good night's sleep. Don't go on and on about that great new place with fabulous music that is teaming with members of the opposite sex who are all trying to get picked up.

220. If you fail a test, and your final exam is cumulative, make SURE you get all the correct answers so you won't miss them on the final.

Pay close attention when your professor goes over the test. If you still have questions afterward, get the answers. Meet with the professor and get them, or get them out of the book. It would be ridiculous to do badly on a test then repeat the very same mistakes on the final.

221. You might be able to pull up a failed test, so earn as many points as you can.

If you fail a test, don't sit around feeling sorry

for yourself. Lick your wounds then get into action!

Go see your professor and tell him/her that you are determined to do better and ask for advice. Ask for extra credit. Develop a plan and don't waver. Become an extremely conscientious student from then on!

If you don't have enough time to pull up a low grade - say you failed your final badly and it dragged your grade way down - you'll just have to learn a hard life lesson. It won't be the end of the world, but make SURE it never happens again.

VII
Taking Tests / Exams

*Most professors like to see an outline.
They know the value of outlines. You can
score points with a good outline, and it
will help you remember everything as well
as organize your writing and make it more
persuasive. Be as neat with your outline
as with your answer itself.*

222. Professors hate sloppy tests. Be neat with everything.

Make sure your professor can read everything
without straining. Write legibly and neatly. Don't
scratch things out if you can avoid it. If a
professor has to strain to read you writing, you
are in trouble, even if it is a single letter he/she
has to struggle to read.

Remember, when professors grade, they look
at a paper from everybody in your class. That
might be 100 tests. But even 25 is a lot for a
professor to grade if it is a lengthy discussion test
or has a lot of short-answer or fill-in-the-blank
questions. If you write poorly or lightly, and the
professor has to wrestle with your writing or can't

see it, you are dead (and you are a dummy!).

223. Consider erasable ink for exams.

I took all my exams with erasable ink. It gave me the authority of ink but the ability to erase and change an answer at will. Erasable ink pens are inexpensive and have an ink eraser on the tip, like a pencil. You can find them anywhere.

Erasable ink is fine for exams but I didn't like it for anything else. It can smudge, but for one blue book test, it is fine.

224. When you are handed your exam and your professor says you can look at it, glance at the *whole* thing, so you know what you are dealing with, then quickly answer all the questions you know.

Note how much time you will have for the different sections based on their point value then jump on the questions you know. Finish the questions you know, quickly, then go back to the ones you will have to struggle with. Make sure you ALWAYS answer the questions you know first, and do them as quickly as possible. Get some points on the board then wrestle with the rest of the test.

225. Make SURE you don't miss any pages or extra credit questions.

One time, somehow, I missed the last page of an exam. I had an "A" on everything leading up to the last page. I was checking over my work when I noticed to my horror I had missed the last page.

I rushed to complete it but it was too late and I ended up, IN UTTER FRUSTRATION, with a B on a test I should have easily made an A on. Always pay attention, especially when first getting your test and glancing over it.

Also, make sure there are no questions on the board or anywhere else, to answer.

226. Make SURE you allot your time correctly.

If the short-answer questions are worth only 10% of the grade and the essay question is worth 90%, then spend no more than 10% of the time on the short-answer questions. In a 50 minute class in which 45 minutes are left after the professor hands out the test, 10% is less than five minutes for the short-answer questions.

Once you finish the 90% essay question, you can go back, if you have time, and change any answers to the short-answer questions that you don't like.

227. Even within sections of an exam, you must be allot your time correctly.

Say you have some multiple-choice questions worth 25% of the grade, and five essay questions worth 75%, of which you must answer three of the five.

In a 50 minute class, you have just over 11 minutes for the multiple-choice questions. Click on your stop watch, or note the time you must switch to the essay questions, then do it.

You will have just over a half hour for the essay questions. You must answer three, so you have just over 11 minutes each, plus it is *always* a good idea to leave yourself a little time to look over your test to make sure you haven't skipped anything or put an answer in the wrong space, etc.

228. Start with the essay question you can answer best and fastest, then go to the one you can answer next best and fastest, then finally the one you have to wrestle with.

Your professor will usually tell you or write on the board how much time is left during an exam, especially toward the end.

Keep an eye on your own watch, anyway, so you know where you stand at all times.

229. Just DON'T get hung-up on a question.

You will know if you are getting hung-up and spending too much time. Your gut will give you a panic reaction, so pay attention to your gut and MOVE ON, then come back to the hard question later.

ALWAYS leave yourself time to at least guess at questions you left blank on the first pass. ALWAYS put something down. NEVER leave a question unanswered.

230. Outline discussion answers in the margin, and be neat.

If a professor tells you not to write in the margin, then don't. Otherwise, outline the answer to a discussion question in the margin.

Most professors like to see an outline. They know the value of outlines. You can score points with a good outline, and it will help you remember everything as well as organize your writing and make it more persuasive. Be as neat with your outline as with your answer itself.

Here's what I do, but you do whatever works for you. If I had to answer a question about Edgar Allan Poe and his Charleston connection, I would form a column in the left-hand margin and put a dash in front of each point I wanted to make:

- Mother performed in Charleston
- U.S. Army as Edgar A. Perry
- Stationed Sullivan's Is., Fort Moultrie
- Gold-Bug, Sullivan's Is.
- Annabel Lee
- Considered himself Southern
- Deaths of beautiful women in his life
- Etc., etc.

Quickly put everything in your outline that occurs to you about a question so you don't miss anything. You can organize your points later by putting numbers next to them or some such method. If something occurs to you when writing, add it immediately to your outline so you don't lose it.

231. Always write things down as they occur to you.

If you think you will simply remember something later, you are wrong. You won't.

This is true about great ideas that occur to you in life. WRITE THEM DOWN and date them the moment you think of them. If you don't, you'll lose most of them.

232. Jot notes in the margin on anything that might help answer a question, but stay neat.

Do not hesitate to help yourself. Write

anything you choose in the margin. Professors usually encourage this. Write neatly. Try to keep your test as neat as possible because a neat test exudes correctness and control, and will impress a professor more than a sloppy test.

233. If you run out of time, make SURE you at least outline all the essay questions. The outline can get you some credit.

For example, if you answer two out of the three required essay questions then run out of time as you start the third, outline it well and do what you can, then flip back and put down an answer for any multiple-choice or short answer questions you skipped.

Put down something for EVERY question. Even guessing on a multiple-choice question with four answers gives you a 25% chance of getting it right; and an even greater chance if you can eliminate an answer or two so that you are only choosing between two answers. You would then have a 50/50 chance of getting it right by purely guessing, just as when guessing at a true/false question.

234. Often the answer to a skipped question can be found in another question later in the test.

If you skip a question, keep it in mind as you take the rest of your test. Sometimes the way a professor poses another question will suggest an answer to your skipped question.

Also, the act of composing answers to short-answer and essay questions will help you remember things, including, sometimes, the answers to skipped questions.

Always think this way.

235. It is best to go with your first answer to a question.

This is especially the case if you have whittled down the possible correct answers, such as when eliminating some multiple-choice options.

One's first answer is based on that intangible, the gut. Any further analysis of a question that you clearly don't know, is a waste of time until you get everything answered that you DO know.

If you have enough time at the end, go back and wrestle with the question, and if you think you have come up with a better answer, then change it.

236. Hold the bull manure to a minimum.

Professors know when you are B.S.-ing on a test and they don't like it. If you don't know the answer to a question, then B.S. artfully and intelligently. Don't just write to be writing.

237. Sometime take-home exams can work you harder than a regular in-class exam.

Take-home exams always sound easy, but one can write and write on a take-home exam. If you have the option of a regular in-class exam, or take-home exam, think hard about it. Think about your specific situation and how well you know the material. You might be better off taking the exam in class and being through with it in 50 minutes rather than spending hours writing and writing on a take-home exam.

Of course, if you don't know the material, then the take-home exam is your best option.

VIII
Papers and Writing

The first lesson: DON'T GET STUCK. If you get stuck, get yourself unstuck quick, any way you can. People get stuck because they act like wimps and whine and stare at the wall and feel sorry for themselves. Don't be a big baby. Fire up your brain! Be a man or a woman! Put some words down on paper! Put some clay on the potter's wheel and get going!

The second lesson: An EXCELLENT method of writing is to write your first draft straight from your brain without stopping to look at your sources. Just write what you know and keep moving as fast as possible. The writing is so much more natural and comes easier than when you refer back, constantly, to books, articles and notes.

238. Anything you have to research and write, you are going to learn well.

If you have a topic you are very interested in, do a paper on it. You will learn the material well and it will be stimulating and fun. You'll learn a lot more than you anticipated.

239. Make sure you understand from your professor the exact way he/she wants your paper written and cited.

Follow the professor's instructions to the letter! Stay close to the length he/she wants. You can go over a little, but never fall short. If you feel like you need to write more, check with your professor first.

Make sure you understand how to cite Internet sources, if they are allowed.

240. Forget "easy." Choose topics that you are dying to learn about. You'll be motivated and enjoy it more.

Don't pick paper topics just because you think they are easy, or because a lot of information is available. You will still have to work hard to write the paper, cite your sources and make a persuasive argument. Why do all that with a subject you don't care about?

Pick something you have a passion for, that you are in a white heat to research and learn about. You'll be highly motivated the whole time. Your mind will work so much better.

241. Consider topics that will help you in other parts of a course, or in a different course.

This is a smart overall strategy, especially for magna cum laude students, because it gives you twice the mileage out of your effort.

If one of your topic selections is related to something you have coming up in another course, then think about writing on it. You will learn it well, and when it comes up in the other course, you will already know it and won't have to spend time learning it, and can NAIL it on the test!

I am NOT encouraging you to write one paper and use it twice. If you choose a topic that you can write on in two courses, then do a good paper in the first, and do a different paper for the second, perhaps more in-depth or from a different angle. You will be writing the second paper with even more authority because you will have learned so much doing the first. And you end up knowing a great deal about the topic, which is exactly what you want, especially for a topic you really care about and might have plans to study in graduate school or elsewhere.

Always think this way.

242. Decide on paper topics as QUICKLY as possible.

The moment your options for paper topics are given to you by your professor, reserve yours! Get one that really fascinates you rather than having to take what's left over!

Also, if you choose a topic early on, you can be thinking about it all the time. If something comes up that can help, you can note it for further research, or research it right then.

Label a manila file folder and start accumulating research, clippings, articles, etc.

Create a directory (folder) on your computer and add things such as computer files, links to helpful websites, images, etc.

243. Once you choose your topic, spend a little time with it as soon as you can and develop at least a tentative research strategy.

Spend a half day with your topic as soon as you can. See what materials are out there. Think about your research approach. Perhaps order books from interlibrary loan. Search the Internet.

Put specific dates on your calendar by which you want to start and finish your research, start writing, produce a draft, and finish.

Just taking action will make you feel good, and what you discover initially will open other doors and get you moving fast.

244. Make SURE the books you need for research are available.

The sooner you can go to your library, and

other libraries you have access to, the more likely that the books you need will be available. Papers are not usually due until later in the semester but DON'T be lulled to sleep!

Make sure you can get EVERY book you need before others beat you to them. This is war! Renew the books if you need to. You don't have to start your paper right away but checking out some books, getting some research out of the way, making copies out of some books, is good.

If you don't get those books, others will, *especially* if other students in the class are writing on the same or similar topics, and you'll be high and dry.

Don't ever be high and dry if you plan to graduate magna cum laude, or if you are hanging by a thread your last semester.

245. Papers can sneak up on you.

That's why it is critical to take control from the beginning.

If you know what you are facing because you decided on a topic early, you can put dates on your calendar by which you want to start and complete various parts of your research and writing.

You will be able to use time efficiently, especially if you need to work during fall or spring break.

246. The worst thing to do is wait until the last minute to start a paper.

There is no possibility the best books will be in the library, and there is a strong possibility there will be NO good books left. You'll get the crumbs. The crumbs won't cut it.

You'll also be under too much pressure at the last minute.

Give yourself plenty of time to write papers. Make sure your self-imposed start dates are on your calendar, and your due date.

Break the work into segments and put segment-start and completion dates on your calendar, such as a date by which you want to finish most of your research, a date for completing the first draft, etc.

Always think this way about papers.

247. For many history, political science and literature courses, a general history fact finder is an invaluable aid.

For quickly verifying names, dates and the details of history, a fact finder is a MUST for your reference collection. Save yourself a lot of time. When something comes up in research and you are not sure of a date or detail, look it up in your fact finder FAST!

I have used *The Great American History Fact-*

Finder for years.[17] It is outstanding and has been very helpful.

There are other general fact finders out there for specific areas of study. Get any of them that will help you.

Never hesitate to buy a reference book for your personal library. They more than pay for themselves in time savings and accurate research. Go to Amazon.com and other book sites and search for anything related to your research.

248. A desk encyclopedia is also valuable.

A good desk encyclopedia takes you beyond a specific fact finder and broadens your research capabilities. I've used *Merriam-Webster's Collegiate Encyclopedia* for years.[18] It is a single large volume and easy to grab off a shelf.

Of course, encyclopedias and fact finders are excellent providers of overviews of a topic, and details here and there, but they are not sources to cite. For your papers, you need to get much deeper into a topic and more specific than the broad details provided by an encyclopedia.

---

[17] Ted Yanak and Pam Cornelison, *The Great American History Fact Finder* (Boston: Houghton Mifflin Company, 1993). One should use the most recent edition possible.
[18] *Merriam-Webster's Collegiate Encyclopedia* (Springfield, MA: Merriam-Webster, Inc. and Encyclopedia Britannica, Inc., 2000). One should use the most recent edition possible.

249. CliffsNotes, SparkNotes or their equivalent can aid in your research, especially if it is literary.

Do not use a study guide instead of reading an assigned book. If you do, you will be cheating yourself. But definitely use study guides to enhance your reading and research.

CliffsNotes, SparkNotes, Monarch Notes (Barnes & Noble) and similar guides are powerful and helpful, and are written by top scholars. They can save you major time by providing such things as background, a chronology, author information and additional resources for your research.

CliffsNotes, SparkNotes, et al., are study enhancements only, and NOT sources to quote from or cite in your paper, though the additional resources they mention probably are.

250. Don't hesitate to Google anything! . . . especially while you are sitting at your desk researching and writing.

ANY question you have about anything, Google it! The answer will usually pop up in nanoseconds.

Make sure the answer is correct. Compare it with the answer in your desktop encyclopedia. Check several other websites to make sure they have the same information. Look for university websites. Encyclopedia Britannica Online is only

$69.95 a year (as of September, 2012). It is always a good, credible source.

251. Wikipedia will usually pop up first or close to first, and it is usually extremely helpful.

Wikipedia is especially helpful with people, events, books, really everything, and they are linked to Wikimedia Commons, which includes *excellent* public domain pictures and documents you can use.[19]

When researching, it is very good and fascinating to be able to look at pictures of people, places, documents, etc., involved with your topic.

Just check behind Wikipedia because it might not have all the information, or the information might be biased or even incorrect.

Look at Wikipedia's sources. Go to some of them.

252. If you are not sure of a spelling, type in what you know and if it is incorrect, usually Google will suggest the correct spelling.

I just type in what I know followed by one space and "def", the first three letters of "definition." Here's an example of what I would

---

[19] Wikimedia Commons homepage states that it is "a database of 16,524,428 freely usable media files to which anyone can contribute." Accessed March 26, 2013, http://commons.wikimedia.org/wiki/Main_Page.

type into the search bar in a browser, or Google toolbar, if I was searching for the spelling or definition of the word, "allure": allure def.

Since browsers guess what you are typing in, they take the "def" to mean "definition" and instantly will give several sites with definitions for the word - sites such as: TheFreeDictionary.com, Merriam-Webster.com, Answers.com, et al.

You can quickly view part of the definitions that are popping up without even clicking on a site, and thus verify that you have the right word and right spelling.

You can do this to verify a definition or find synonyms or antonyms. The definition websites will give you links to synonyms, etc., or you can do another search by typing in the word followed by a space then "synonym," or whatever you need.

The Internet is REAL POWER these days! Just check everything with multiple sites to make sure you have the right spelling and/or definition or whatever you are looking for.

253. You can use a thesaurus to find a correct spelling if you are not at your computer.

For example, if you can't find the word "plagiarize" in the dictionary and are trying to confirm its spelling, look up a synonym for plagiarize, such as "copy." Under copy, one of the suggestions in my Roget's International Thesaurus Fourth Edition is "imitate," and one of the words listed under imitate is "plagiarize."

254. Read primary sources as often as possible when writing history papers.

Primary sources are the original documents from the past such as the Declaration of Independence, John Locke's *Two Treatises of Government*, the Magna Carta, Thomas Jefferson's Kentucky Resolutions, Karl Marx's *Das Kapital*, newspapers, government documents, the records of Congress, court records, etc. Also, the letters and diaries written by people in the past.

255. Secondary sources are interpretations of history by later scholars.

Some scholars are outstanding. Some are pathetic. A LOT are politically correct, interpreting history the way they need to interpret it to get tenure.

Make sure you know the reputation of historians you are reading. You need to know how credible they are, and their biases. Unless a historian is well known, do some research to see what other things he/she has published or is known for.

Do NOT rely on somebody else's

interpretation of the past. Go to primary sources yourself. Read the letters, diaries and documents. Make up your own mind.

256. Be aware of the scourge of political correctness on scholarship and free speech.

Since the rise of political correctness, many events of the past are interpreted according to the latest political fashion instead of the standards that existed at the time.

This is kin to another scourge, advocacy journalism, in which some "journalists" apply their morals, or lack thereof, to the news, and report on it that way rather than giving us the impartial facts. This is another reason why Americans hold the press in such low esteem these days.

Political correctness makes history little more than propaganda, just as advocacy journalism turns the front page into the editorial page.

257. You can not possibly understand history by using today's standards to judge the past.

You HAVE to look at the past the way the people who lived in the past looked at it. That's how you understand the past.

258. Political correctness is ignorance and leads to a total lack of historical understanding.

You can't define the past by snippets of acceptable history here and there.

For example, the South gets beat up all the time for slavery but most slave traders were New Englanders who made huge fortunes in the process. An argument can be made that the entire infrastructure of the Old North was built on profits from slave traders such as Boston's Peter Faneuil of Faneuil Hall fame. That's why most Northerners had NO problem with slavery. Less than 5% were abolitionists, and ironically, many abolitionists didn't like slavery because they didn't like blacks and did not want to associate with them.

One such person was Rep. David Wilmot, Democrat from Pennsylvania. Wilmot sponsored the *Wilmot Proviso* to keep slavery out of the West, though his real goal was to keep blacks out of the West, and he admitted it. Abraham Lincoln also said, in the *Lincoln-Douglas Debates*, that he wanted the West reserved for white people from all over the earth. No blacks allowed.

While many say that slavery was the cause of the War Between the States, Abraham Lincoln said it was not. Before the war, Lincoln favored the first 13th Amendment to the U.S. Constitution which would have left black people

in slavery FOREVER, even beyond the reach of
Congress. That amendment passed in the
Northern Congress after Southerners seceded,
and was ratified by some Northern States before
the war began and made it moot.

There are breaths of fresh air here and there
such as the 2005 book *Complicity, How the North
Promoted, Prolonged, and Profited from Slavery*,
by Anne Farrow, Joel Lang, and Jenifer Frank of
The Hartford Courant.[20]

History is always more complex than the self-
moralizing, politically correct want you to believe.

**259. Southern history as it is taught today is
a "cultural and political atrocity," and students
are being CHEATED.**

Esteemed historian, Eugene D. Genovese, who
passed away September 26, 2012, was disgusted
with the way Southern history is taught today. He
writes:

> To speak positively about any part of this
> Southern tradition is to invite charges of
> being a racist and an apologist for
> slavery and segregation. **We are
> witnessing a cultural and political
> atrocity** — an increasingly successful

---

[20] Anne Farrow, Joel Lang, and Jenifer Frank, *Complicity,
How the North Promoted, Prolonged, and Profited from
Slavery* (New York: Ballantine Books, 2005).

> campaign by the media and an academic
> elite to strip young white Southerners,
> and arguably black Southerners as well,
> of their heritage, and therefor, their
> identity. They are being taught to forget
> their forebears or to remember them
> with shame. (my emphasis).[21]

A perfect example is William Gilmore Simms. According to Edgar Allan Poe, Simms was the greatest American writer of the 19th century. Simms wrote 82 book-length works including 20 that are very important in American history and literature. He understood the publishing industry of that era better than anybody and wrote about it. He chronicled American westward expansion when Alabama was the edge of the West; and his Revolutionary War novels, set in and around Charleston, are exciting, vivid history as it happened. Simms was a nationally recognized expert on the Revolution. He wrote dramatic, historically accurate scenes of when the British conquered Charleston and marched in, and when they lost the war and marched out, and everything in between. Simms also knew the local Indians extremely well and much of what is known about them is in his work, including their

---

[21] Eugene D. Genovese, *The Southern Tradition, The Achievement and Limitations of an American Conservatism* (Cambridge, MA and London: Harvard University Press, 1994), xi-xii.

languages. There is a bust of William Gilmore Simms in White Point Gardens at The Battery in Charleston, high up on a beautiful pedestal.

But Simms is not studied because he was a slaveholder.

260. Young students of history and literature should examine everything.

Don't assume the War Between the States was about slavery when the economy of the North collapsed into near-anarchy as the Southern States seceded. The Northern economy was dependent on manufacturing and selling to its captive Southern market, and without the South, Northern factories stood idle.

The South, on the other hand, seceded and was ecstatic at finally having control of its own economy. Southerners had always wanted free trade and immediately wrote into their constitution a prohibition on protective tariffs.

The North, at the same time, passed the astronomical Morrill Tariff, which made goods entering the North 40% to 70% higher. This was aimed at Southerners, as all the antebellum tariffs had been, so European goods would be too costly for Southerners to afford and they would have to buy from the North at higher prices.

But with the South out of the Union, Southerners were no longer obligated to pay

Northern tariffs, and suddenly, much-sought-after Europeans goods were far less expensive for Southerners than Northern goods.

261. Those historians with a vested interest in maintaining that slavery caused the war are not telling you the truth. They are cheating you out of understanding much of American history.

Economic factors were HUGE in 1861 just as they are today. The collapse of the Northern economy, alone, was enough for Abraham Lincoln to want war.

Just look at our own era. We have been quite willing to go to war to maintain the free flow of oil from the Middle East because a disruption of the oil supply means economic hardship, even collapse. Gas prices would soar and cause the price of everything else to jump off the scale. Business would grind to a halt. People would lose their jobs and not have money to feed their families. They would be angry and in the street.

You can imagine what would happen if supplies of oil to the United States were cut off abruptly and completely! Fortunately, that would never happen because we would go to war to prevent it. We have.

But, "abruptly" and "completely" is exactly what happened to the North when the South seceded and the Northern Congress passed the Morrill Tariff. Instantly, it would cost the rest of the world 40% to 70% more to do business with the North, so NOBODY wanted to.

The rest of the world was beating a path to the South where protective tariffs were unconstitutional and where there was a huge market for goods, and that market was wealthy because it controlled King Cotton, which had been 60% of U.S. exports alone in 1861.

The North had shot itself in the leg with the Morrill Tariff — actually, it had shot itself in the head. Northern greed and mismanagement made the economic destruction of the North inevitable, and Northern leaders were in a panic.

Don't take my word for it. Read the words of ALL Northern newspaper editors after January, 1861, when it became apparent that the North needed the South, but the South did not need the North. Northern editors were not thinking about slavery. They were thinking about their own wealth and economy, and they were all petrified. War was preferable for them just as the disruption of oil made war preferable for us.

An excellent two-volume work makes Northern newspaper editors easy to study: *Northern Editorials on Secession*, edited by Dr. Howard Cecil Perkins, Volumes I and II, over 1,100 pages, a 1964 reprint published by Peter Smith, Gloucester, Massachusetts. *Northern Editorials on Secession* was originally published in 1942 by the American Historical

Association.[22]

262. Another major issue was unfair taxation — British taxes were a huge issue in 1776 but were minuscule compared to what the South was paying in 1861.

For Southerners, 1861 was 1776 all over.

Southerners were paying 3/4ths of the Federal Government's taxes, but 3/4ths of the tax money was being spent in the North. Robert Toombs famously called it a suction pump sucking wealth out of the South and depositing it in the North.

The level of "taxation without representation" that led to the Revolutionary War was minuscule compared to what the South was suffering prior to seceding.

The point is that politically correct historians who tell you that it is cut and dried that slavery caused the War Between the States are being dishonest. Many are lazy because they have not been required, by vigorous academic debate, to look into other issues - especially economics. Many don't understand economics, and why should they bother. It is too easy for them to play up slavery and call anyone who disagrees a racist.

However, we have fought two Gulf Wars in

---

[22] Howard Cecil Perkins, ed., *Northern Editorials on Secession*, Volumes I and II (1942; reprint, Gloucester, MA: Peter Smith, 1964) by permission of The American Historical Association and Appleton-Century-Crofts, Inc.

our own times to guarantee the free flow of oil because a disruption would cause an economic meltdown and untold problems. No government is willing to risk that because history has shown us that an economic collapse will get out of control and lead to a collapse of the government itself, and anarchy. War is preferable.

It's true today and it was true in 1861.

So, look deeply into the entire picture and assume nothing.

263. Be a scholar.

Read primary sources. Read the words of the people of the past, their speeches, newspapers, diaries, laws and documents. Pay attention to secondary sources from historians you trust, and give no credence to those you don't. That's fair and responsible. In your writing, debunk the scholars you disagree with, and tell why they are wrong.

264. Write what you want.

Don't let political correctness chill free speech and intimidate you into not writing on a topic that interests you. Talk to your professor. The best professors will encourage you.

And if one discourages you, find a way around him/her by approaching the topic from a different angle. If he/she brings up some historian who goes against your conclusions, then YOU bring up two who support them. History should always be a vigorous debate.

Do exhaustive research and a thoughtful analysis and document everything properly. Argue with power, vigor, confidence, clearly and persuasively. Do NOT use today's standards, or lack thereof, to judge the people of the past. Understand how the people of the past viewed their lives and times, and what their standards were, and why.

That's what real scholarship is about.

265. Research for papers is why you need to be on great terms with EVERYBODY in the library.

People who become research librarians gravitate to libraries because they love reading, knowledge, books, periodicals, research, the quiet atmosphere of learning in the library, and helping students. That's the mission in life of a research librarian so don't ever hesitate to call on one.

Make friends with them. Make friends with EVERYBODY in the library. If you see any of them out somewhere, buy them a beer. I can assure you it will be worth it.

A librarian or library worker who likes you can do all kind of things for you. Say you needed to renew a book but have already renewed it too many times. A librarian who likes you might be able to correct that situation.

Say you need more than the limit of books you can check out. A librarian might be able to override that too.

Don't take advantage of the system, but there will be times when you need a favor and you can get it if you have cultivated a good relationship with everybody at the library.

266. When researching, it is often good to start with an encyclopedia article as an overview.

Do a Google search and see what is online. Wikipedia will almost certainly pop up. Make sure it is corroborated by other credible sites such as Encyclopedia Britannica Online. Print the Wikipedia and/or Britannica article so you'll have it at your fingertips.

Look at the sources used by an article's author and perhaps examine some of those sources yourself. Always note the encyclopedia publisher and volume information in case you end up citing the article, though encyclopedia articles are not the best things to cite. They are too common.

Encyclopedias are fabulous overviews, but when doing research, use specific sources and go deep into them if necessary.

267. Examine the bibliography or works cited section in articles and books in which you are doing research. They will suggest other sources.

Oftentimes, a book is not that good, or you disagree with the conclusions, but the bibliography IS good. You can examine the same sources used by a scholar with whom you disagree, and come up with completely different conclusions.

268. Look for additional sources of information on people and topics you are studying.

Search every library you have access to online. Search online journals and databases through your school library.

Search the Internet itself. Just make sure anything you read is credible. Also, make sure you get the information you need to be able to cite a website correctly. Many scholarly and encyclopedia web sites will tell you how to cite them, though you should stay away from encyclopedias as sources in papers.

As stated, encyclopedias are great places to *start* research and as overviews. Once you know where you are going, go find more specific sources than encyclopedias.

Ask a reference librarian for help. *Don't hesitate* to ask a reference librarian anything. They are glad to help. That's what they are there for. Remember, the only dumb question is the one that doesn't get asked!

269. Of course, NEVER have the TV on or music playing when writing.

Writing demands focus, concentration and free thought. You want to be able to think about things – thoroughly – that occur to you as you write. You want to look things up and make additional notes to follow up on later.

270. Do what a lot of writers do to improve their writing: Read what other writers say about writing.

It's fascinating, enjoyable, and one always learns a great deal. Read what the writers you admire most say about the craft. Go to Barnes & Noble or Books-A-Million and browse the writing section and magazines on writing.

Go to Amazon and other websites and search for books on writing.

Read a lot. That's what all writers do. Read voraciously. Think about the style of what you are reading.

Ask your professor to recommend things that will help your writing.

271. There is a rhythm and balance to good prose.

Poetry is not the only thing rhythmic. Prose is too. Good prose flows easily, and is not jerky or hard to read. The sentences do not sound awkward. Good prose should be invisible to the reader because a movie is playing in the reader's mind. The reader sees the action, not the words.

272. The best writing is easy to read.

Don't think for a second that big words or wordy sentences make good writing. It is the opposite – common words and shorter, direct sentences – make powerful writing.

Use mostly nouns and verbs.

Use the active voice and not passive. The active is much more vigorous.

Always be aware of moving your argument along as fast as you can because people are smart and easily bored, especially professors. You want to capture and hold their minds with your writing. You want to take them somewhere and NOT let them go until you are ready to let them go.

273. Newspaper-style writing is powerful and effective. Here's good advice from Ernest Hemingway and Professor Strunk.

Newspaper writing is easy-to-read and meant

to relay information fast and clearly. The best writing, even scholarly, should also move fast for the reader and be easily understood, which makes it powerful.

Writing should never be flat. All writing should have a force and clarity to it. That's why the emphasis from Professor Strunk, Stephen King, William Zinsser and everybody else is on the active voice and not passive. Ideally, you want the reader to have a movie playing in his/her head and not even see the words.

Here's Ernest Hemingway's handwritten note on writing:

> Use short sentences, use short first paragraphs, use vigorous English. Be positive. Never use old slang, and eliminate every superfluous word.[23]

In other words, write the way the quotation above is written!

The quotation above comes from *The Kansas City Star Copy Style*, a 1917 guide sheet for new reporters. It was probably used by Hemingway

---

[23] I saw this quotation at an exhibit of photographs of Ernest Hemingway, and of Charleston, South Carolina, by famed photographer *Walker Evans*. The photographs were on display at Gibbes Museum of Art in Charleston and I saw them on February 2, 2006. I could not resist copying down Hemingway's powerful words! See note 24 for more on Hemingway and *The Kansas City Star Copy Style* sheet.

when he was a new police and emergency-room reporter for the *Kansas City Star* at age 18. A few years later, he said about those rules:

> Those were the best rules
> I ever learned for the business of
> writing . . . I've never forgotten
> them. . . .[24]

Hemingway's advice is incredibly similar to Professor Strunk's in *The Elements of Style*:

> Omit needless words. Vigorous
> writing is concise. A sentence should
> contain no unnecessary words, a
> paragraph no unnecessary sentences,
> for the same reason that a drawing
> should have no unnecessary lines
> and a machine no unnecessary parts.
> This requires not that the writer
> make all sentences short, or avoid all
> detail and treat subjects only in
> outline, but that every word tell.[3]

---

[24] Jim Fisher, (*Star* columnist), "Ernest Hemingway and *The Kansas City Star* / Of '*Star* Style' and a reporter named Hemingway", *The Kansas City Star* website, accessed March 26, 2013, http://www.kcstar.com/hemingway/ hem3.shtml. There is much good information on Hemingway and *The Kansas City Star* on their website.

274. Reread (or read) E. B. White's essay on writing in *The Elements of Style*: "An Approach to Style (With a List of Reminders)."

Here's an excerpt previously mentioned in Chapter I but worth repeating:

> Who can confidently say what ignites
> a certain combination of words,
> causing them to explode in the mind?
> Who knows why certain notes in
> music are capable of stirring the
> listener deeply, though the same
> notes slightly rearranged are
> impotent? . . . The preceding
> chapters (in *The Elements of Style*)
> contain instructions drawn from
> established English usage; this one
> contains advice drawn from a
> writer's experience of writing.[4]

White goes on to say that a person's writing "style" is a mystery, then he gives us 21 powerful pieces of writing advice, in Strunkian style. In the book, each topic is followed by a discussion, from two paragraphs to a page-and-a-half, long:

1. Place yourself in the background.
2. Write in a way that comes naturally.
3. Work from a suitable design.
4. Write with nouns and verbs.
5. Revise and rewrite.

6. Do not overwrite.

7. Do not overstate.

8. Avoid the use of qualifiers.

9. Do not affect a breezy manner.

10. Use orthodox spelling.

11. Do not explain too much.

12. Do not construct awkward adverbs.

13. Make sure the reader knows who is speaking.

14. Avoid fancy words.

15. Do not use dialect unless your ear is good.

16. Be clear.

17. Do not inject opinion.

18. Use figures of speech sparingly.

19. Do not take shortcuts at the cost of clarity.

20. Avoid foreign languages.

21. Prefer the standard to the offbeat.[25]

275. Ask your professor if he/she has an example of an "A" paper like the one you are required to write. Do this for any paper you have to write in any course.

My professor for English 650 posted three excellent examples of the annotated bibliographical essay we were required to write, and he encouraged us to examine them in detail. They were written by outstanding students in previous semesters. We were able to go to our

---

[25] Strunk and White, *The Elements of Style*, 70-85.

professor's website and download them.

Having those examples of the right form and style, as well as what the professor considered an excellent paper, was extremely helpful.

For any course, even 100-level undergraduate courses, ask your professor if he/she has an example of an A paper you can use as a guide.

276. If you know what you want to say, and you have done good research, your paper will burst out of you.

And that's what you want! It will flow better, read better, and be far more natural. It will be more passionate. You'll automatically emphasize the most important things, and put other things in perspective.

When I write a paper, I do so much research that my head becomes packed full of information and I reach a critical mass, and, at that point, am ready to start writing. I create at least a basic outline, then the writing bursts out of me like water breaking through a dam. I always write more persuasively and naturally in these situations, rather than jerkily starting and stopping.

Just gather your research materials, do an outline and start writing.

You can alter your course as you go. You can add or take away items away later, but start writing and get that first draft out of you as quickly as possible.

277. Once you start writing, stay focused like a laser.

It is easy to deviate from your topic. DON'T. It will waste huge amounts of time if you start researching and writing on ancillary topics that you will likely cut later anyway.

It is hard to stay focused, sometimes, but you CAN'T be all over the place with research and writing. You'll water down your topic and never finish your paper.

Write an entire draft as focused as humanly possible, then, if you need to expand on some aspect, do it.

278. Write your first draft in a white heat . . . or not.

My preference is to follow an outline and write, write, write, once research is mostly done! I want to put clay on the potter's wheel. I can shape it later. I don't let anything stop me, especially not grammar or spelling. I can edit later. As I go along, I make additional notes when things occur to me.

This is my style. You might have a method that works better for you, and that is fine.

I like the white heat style because good

writing happens when one is thinking about the points they want to make, and not about each word or each sentence. Make your points with clarity and organization but also passion. Let your enthusiasm show in your writing.

The other side of the coin is that if you are bored, that will come out too.

It always goes back to your paper topic. If you have chosen something that fires you up, something you are really interested in, your paper will write itself.

If you picked a topic because it looked easy and you could care less about it, your paper will show that too.

For me, white heat allows me to maintain my energy and focus in the first draft, then I can shape it up later.

279. Develop your own style of writing. Do what works for you.

There is no hard, fast, right or wrong way to do many things in life. Everybody is different. Each person has different strengths and weaknesses to play up or play down. Each person has his/her own interpretation of events, and different things to say. Each person is capable of a unique style.

Find yours. Do what works for you, as long as you don't cheat or break the law.

Think outside the box. Experiment. Be dynamic and authoritative.

Think about the things you read that are interesting and well-written. Use them as examples.

The more papers you write, the better you will be with research and writing. Embrace the work. You'll be better prepared for graduate school and the working world. Both demand clear, powerful writing based on good research.

280. You must put most of the clay on the potter's wheel before you can shape it.

Put it up there in the general shape you think you want, then other things will suggest themselves as you write, and first thing you know, you have a nicely sculpted piece.

You can't do a thing until you finish your draft, and you shouldn't even try. The draft has a life of its own. I have written drafts then later moved whole sections around, or eliminated whole sections.

Your draft will show you what works and what doesn't. It will be obvious, especially after you sleep on it. You'll then know how to complete your paper.

281. If you get stuck, you must quickly get UNstuck.

Don't ever waste time in life. Time is all you have. You can not reclaim wasted time. It's lost forever. Time that is wasted could better have been used in other pursuits including entertaining yourself. So, make a philosophical choice as early as possible in life to never waste time.

If you get stuck or can't start a paper, then struggle and be hard on yourself until you break out of it. Do something. Write something. Usually your outline will keep you on track.

Once you have started, you will automatically be able to continue, and soon you'll begin picking up momentum.

282. I almost had a disaster in English 650 because I got stuck.

It was fall of 2002. I was a middle-age working student in graduate school at the University of Charleston, the joint program of the College of Charleston and The Citadel. I was working toward a masters in English. I was taking *Literary Research* under Professor James M. Hutchisson, an outstanding writer and professor at The Citadel. Our main course paper, which counted one-third of our grade, was an annotated bibliographical essay. I needed a mid-B in the course to be fully-admitted to the English M.A. program since I had been a History major.

I had chosen a subject on which my professor has written books and was unquestionably an expert. It bothered me a little that my professor knew my topic inside and out, but I was extremely interested in the topic. It was the Charleston Literary Renaissance of the 1920s, which included such brilliant people as DuBose Heyward, author of the novel, *Porgy*, on which the opera, *Porgy and Bess*, is based. In fact, *Porgy and Bess* was composed in the summer of 1934 by George Gershwin with help from DuBose Heyward on Folly Beach, one island over from James Island, where I live.

I had done a ton of research but the deadline was on top of me – the next day, in fact – but I was stuck and just could not get started. I had so much material before me it was preventing me from focusing. I'd start, then tear it up, start again, tear again, start, tear, start, tear. I was up most of the night then decided, around 5 a.m., to get an extension so I'd have more time to write my paper. I hated to do it because I needed to study for other exams.

I e-mailed my professor, making the case that I had had marital problems and had gotten separated and it had proved too much of a distraction. I went to bed thinking I would wake up a few hours later, check my e-mail and have the extension I wanted.

Not hardly! My professor was unmoved. He said to turn in what I had and we'd go from there.

Well, I had nothing. I had a lot of excellent research. Tons of it! And I had all my sources from months of work spread out around my house, but I had no paper. I didn't even have a draft. This was 8:30 a.m. and I had until 5 p.m., when class started, to turn in a completed semester-length bibliographical essay that counted one-third of my grade in a 600 level graduate course in which I had to make a mid-B to be fully-admitted into the English M.A. program. I had an A in the course so far. Talk about pressure!

I got to work, fast! I mean I was moving like lighting. I had formed opinions from research. I focused on my outline then started writing. I wrote in a white heat. I had no time to look anything up other than to verify citation. I wrote and wrote. I wrote naturally and let it flow out of my mind. I had to go with what was in my brain, and I left nothing out.

I pressed all day as hard as I could without stopping, shaving, showering. I barely ate. I realized I would not get to class on time but I thought I could get to class before it was over and turn in my paper.

Right as class time was ending, I took off for The Citadel, walked into class and nobody was there. I was shocked! The class had been dismissed early.

Went to my professor's office and he was not there, so I slid my paper under his door then walked to the library and called him. Luckily, I got him and told him my paper was under his door, thus it was being turned in on time. He was cool and appreciative and that made me, finally, start feeling relieved.

I felt like I had written a pretty good bibliographical essay, all things considered. I had reached the obligatory length of 25 pages. Knowing that I could have failed the course by losing letter grades for not turning in a paper on time and I could have been kicked out of graduate school, I did not feel bad that I had violated every rule I know by not producing a draft much quicker in the process and by not sleeping on my final writing for two or three days.

But it was one of those things that happens in life when a person gets stuck in an impossible situation and has to do the best he or she can. I had.

I ended up making an 84 on the paper, which is almost unbelievable since it was written on three hours sleep the very day it had to be turned in. If I had not done good research and had all my sources right there in front of me, and if I had not had good methods for writing and citing material, I would have been dead.

283. It did drop my "A" in the course down to a "B+", but it taught me two VALUABLE lessons.

The first lesson: DON'T GET STUCK. If you get stuck, get yourself unstuck quick, any way you can. People get stuck because they act like wimps and whine and stare at the wall and feel sorry for themselves. Don't be a big baby. Fire up your brain! Be a man or a woman! Put some words down on paper! Put some clay on the potter's wheel and get going!

The second lesson: An EXCELLENT method of writing is to write your first draft straight from your brain without stopping to look at your sources. Just write what you know and keep moving as fast as possible. The writing is so much more natural and comes easier than when you refer back, constantly, to books, articles and notes.

You can go back later and check everything thoroughly and correct any errors and add additional material or take some out; but your basic paper will have been written in a clear, natural, free-flowing style, and it will serve as a framework for your final paper that you turn in. It will be as if you had written a letter to a friend trying to convince your friend of something. It will be more persuasive, and that's what you want.

If I had had time to sleep on my paper and polish it over a couple days, I would have had a pretty good paper. But at least I was not crushed by the situation, and I learned two extremely valuable lessons.

284. Sleep on any kind of writing, ALWAYS.

Give yourself at least one night to sleep on anything you have written. Wake up the next morning, read what you have written, and edit it. *Undoubtedly*, you'll catch a few little things such as a better word to use here and there, removal/insertion of a comma, or something that was not capitalized.

The *best* thing to do is complete your final draft two or three days, or more, before you have to turn it in. That way you can wake up two or three mornings and reread and reedit your paper.

I can not begin to tell you how many times I've had to rush to turn in a paper without being able to sleep on it, and the moment after turning it in, I'd find a word that could have been more powerful, or a correctly spelled word used incorrectly, such as "to" for "too," or "not" when it should have been "note." Talk about frustrating!

285. Never do final editing on anything that is hand-written, if you can help it.

The hand-written word looks entirely different from the printed word. It is always best to edit "printed" words. Always type your hand-written sheets into your word processor, then edit in your word processor, or print and edit.

You can then transcribe your edits back into your word processor, and print the revised document.

286. It's a good idea to do final editing from printed pages and not the computer screen, if you have time.

Words and sentences on the computer screen have a different impact than words and sentences on paper. Since you will be turning in a printed paper, then edit from printed pages, if possible.

You can finish your final draft, print it then edit directly on your printout.

Then, transcribe your edits back into your computer's word processing program, and print the revised paper.

I know there are often time constraints and this might be a luxury you can't afford. If that is the case, fine. Do the best you can.

But it is good to look at, and edit from, exactly what your professor will see.

287. For a book review, read the book thoroughly, take notes, underline, highlight and tag pages as you read.

Have your way with the book!

Make sure you read the Introduction and any other front material closely, including Acknowledgments. You never know where you will find information you need or can use.

Always read footnotes/endnotes. I like footnotes because one can glance down and read them right then without having to flip to the back, but if you have a book with endnotes, then tag the section in the back or put a little clamp on it so you can get to it with as little disruption in reading as possible. Definitely read footnotes/endnotes as you go along.

With endnotes, you might consider making a copy of the endnote section of the book and stapling it together so you have it at your fingertips as you read. This is a good idea.

Any notes you take in a notebook, be sure and write a page number by them so you can refer back to that page in the book quickly. DO write down things that occur to you as you read, especially things you want to point out in your review.

Follow your professor's instructions to the letter as to the format of your review. See if your professor has an example of a good review you can have or at least look at. It is extremely helpful to be able to see style of citation as well as what your professor considers a well-written paper.

288. You might want to read what others have said about the book. Or not.

If you don't want anybody else's opinion to influence your thoughts, then DON'T look at what anybody else has written.

However, certain kinds of reviews and papers are best written using many other sources. Make your mind up based on your assignment, feelings and style.

289. Always cite your sources and record bibliographical information as you go along.

Whether you are using a numbered footnote/endnote system, or a parenthetical in-text system of citation, do it as you go along. Never wait until the end of a paper to go back and cite sources. It is *way* easier to at least copy down the information you will need for a footnote/endnote and bibliographical entry as you work. Then, when you are finished writing, your citation will be finished too (except for perhaps putting it into proper form).

Citing sources as you write will make your paper more accurate. You aren't likely to miss anything if you cite it the moment you write about it.

Many word processors do footnotes/endnotes and will automatically number them for you. Word processors can also do a bibliography or works cited page, indexes, etc. For information, just search your word processor's help index.

If you are using a numbered footnote/endnote system in which you have to manually input the number of the footnote or endnote, then just put a couple asterisks in place of the number as you go along. Once you're finished, and know the order of all your notes, you can number them then.

290. Popular styles of citation are MLA, APA, Chicago Style and Turabian Style, though there are numerous others depending on the field.

Ask your professor what style he/she wants you to use.

Briefly, MLA (Modern Language Association) is popular in the humanities and when writing about literature and language, especially English. For more information: http://www.MLA.org/style.[26]

APA (American Psychological Association) is popular in fields such as the social sciences, economics and business. For more information: http://en.wikipedia.org/wiki/APA_style.[27]

Chicago Style, based on *The Chicago Manual*

---

[26] MLA (Modern Language Association) citation information on their website, accessed March 27, 2013, http://www.MLA.org/style.

[27] APA (American Psychological Association) citation information on Wikipedia, accessed March 27, 2013, http://en.wikipedia.org/wiki/APA_style.

of Style, is popular for writers and publishers in general, and it is used by several disciplines including History and some Social Sciences. For more information: http://www.chicagomanualofstyle.org/ tools_citationguide.html.[28]

Turabian Style is close to Chicago Style but focuses on student papers. For more information: en.wikipedia.org/wiki/A_Manual_for_Writers_of_ Research_Papers,_Theses,_and_Dissertations.[29]

291. The information needed for a bibliographical or works cited entry is contained in footnotes/endnotes, and vice versa. Here's a Chicago Style example.

If there is a full bibliographical entry, such as this one:

DeRosa, Marshall L. *The Confederate Constitution of 1861, An Inquiry into American Constitutionalism.* Columbia, MO: University of Missouri Press, 1991.

---

[28] Chicago Style (*The Chicago Manual of Style*) citation information on their website, accessed March 27, 2013, http://www.chicagomanualofstyle.org/ tools_citationguide.html.

[29] Turabian Style citation information on Wikipedia, accessed March 27, 2013, en.wikipedia.org/wiki/ A_Manual_for_Writers_of_Research_Papers,_Theses,_and_ Dissertations.

THEN

the first footnote/endnote can look like this:

> [1] DeRosa, *The Confederate Constitution of 1861*, 1.

If there is not a full bibliographical entry, then the first footnote/endnote needs to look like this:

> [1] Marshall L. DeRosa, *The Confederate Constitution of 1861, An Inquiry into American Constitutionalism* (Columbia, MO: University of Missouri Press, 1991), 1.

And subsequent footnotes/endnotes should look like the short one above.

Frankly, I think it is better, even if you have a bibliography, to use the longer footnote first, in the text, then use the shorter form for subsequent uses. It is more informative for the reader as he/she reads. The reader doesn't have to flip to the back to look at the bibliography to get the information. It is right there.

Make SURE you follow the style your professor tells you to follow. He/she will help you with citation and probably give you examples or tell you where you can find examples. Librarians can also help you.

Just make sure footnotes/endnotes are

numbered correctly, and make sure the bibliography or works cited information is in alphabetical order.

Word processors usually have an "insert footnote" command that will automatically number footnotes for you throughout a document as you work. It will also drop you to the bottom of the page so you can type out the actual footnote. Any changes to one footnote automatically update the rest. Atlantis, which I use, has an excellent "insert footnote" command.

Search in your word processor's help index for "footnotes" and read everything about them. It will be worth your while!

292. If your word processor won't help with the bibliography, simply paste the citation information at the end of your paper as you write.

By pasting the citation information at the end of your paper as you work, you will accumulate the information needed for your bibliography or works cited page. You will then only need to put it in the proper form, and alphabetize.

293. Save your paper's word processing file REGULARLY as you work! The keystrokes are simple and fast.

Hold down the Control key and hit the "s" for

Save. You file is immediately saved with the file name you opened, and in the folder you last saved it in.

You can also use the "Save As" command, which is usually under the pull-down File menu at the top of your word processor screen. The "Save As" command will enable you to check your file name and where it is being saved. You can also change the file name and where it is being saved, and you can change the type of file that is being saved, e.g., you can change a .doc to a .rtf file, etc.

294. Always create TWO files of anything you are working on in case you accidentally delete the main one, or the main one becomes corrupted. Here's an easy way to do it. *(This is a repeat from Chapter 1, but worth repeating here).*

Say you are working on a paper for a Shakespeare class using MS Word or some other word processor. You might name your file: Shakespeare301Paper.doc.

Now, ALSO save it as Shakespeare301Paper-BACKUP.doc.

It's so easy and you always have two files and that is important. Files get corrupted, or you can mess them up yourself easy enough.

The best way to follow this method is to do this: Save the main file – Shakespeare301Paper.doc – then click File, and Save As.

The file name you just saved –
Shakespeare301Paper – should still be right there
in front of you, and highlighted.

Click behind Shakespeare301Paper so that
you can add to the file name, then add the dash
and BACKUP. I like putting BACKUP in caps
because it makes the backup file stand out.

Then click Save, and you are done. You will
now have two identical files:
Shakespeare301Paper.doc *and*
Shakespeare301Paper-BACKUP.doc. (the file
name suffix, such as .doc, is added automatically
by Word and other word processors).

If an evil computer gremlin corrupts your
Shakespeare301Paper.doc file, all you have to do
is open Shakespeare301Paper-BACKUP.doc, then
click File, Save as, and save it as
Shakespeare301Paper.doc, which was your
original file before the gremlin got it.

You would then have restored your main
Shakespeare paper file, and be back to having two
perfect files.

If you did not have a backup, you would be
DEAD.

**295. Save individual files you are working on
to both your master folder AND the master folder
backup on your flash drive.** *(This is a repeat from
Chapter 1, but worth repeating here).*

Save your files *frequently* as you work. I used

plural – files – because you should be saving *two* files every time you save. Remember the example above: Shakespeare301Paper.doc *and* Shakespeare301Paper-BACKUP.doc.

ALWAYS do this.

At the end of your work session, after you have saved both files for the last time, change the folder you are saving to ⋯ to your master folder backup on your flash drive, and save both files there.

OR, you can copy both files from your master folder in My Documents, to the master folder on your flash drive

Whatever you do, it's BEST to have a rigid routine when it comes to saving and backing up your work. ALWAYS think about what you are doing and be conscious of what you are doing! It is incredibly easy to copy an old file over a new one, and if you do that, you wipe out all your work for that day, or worse.

296. Also back up your work to a CD or DVD, something that is separate from your computer in case your computer blows up. *(This is a repeat from Chapter 1, but worth repeating here).*

If your house takes a direct lighting strike, even a UPS might not save your computer, and you could lose even backups on flash drives.

Copy your master folder to a CD or DVD regularly, then remove the CD or DVD from the computer. Put it in a protective plastic CD case.

You can also copy your master folder to an extra flash drive or two, then remove them. That will give you another layer of protection.

297. Consider subscribing to a service that backs up your files automatically. *(This is a repeat from Chapter 1, but worth repeating here).*

Do some research. One service recommended by Kim Komando is www.Carbonite.com, but there are others.[11]

298. BE EXTREMELY CAREFUL when copying files and folders. You can destroy all your work if you aren't. *(This is a repeat from Chapter 1, but worth repeating here).*

Make SURE you don't copy an old file over a new one. That's why I put "BACKUP" in caps.

When you start working each day, just make sure you start with a file in your master folder in My Documents. You might need to go to a course folder in your master folder. As long as you always start in My Documents, you can rest assured that your most current work is always in your master folder in My Documents.

299. A deleted file will stay in your Recycle Bin until you use the "Empty the Recycle Bin" command. *(This is a repeat from Chapter 1, but worth repeating here).*

A deleted file is stored in your Recycle Bin in case you need to restore it from there, but don't depend on your Recycle Bin for anything. It is a last ditch save option.

As stated, always make two copies, at least, of every important file AND save them to your master folder AND your backup master folder.

300. It's worth repeating: NEVER, EVER turn in an essay you picked up on the Internet as your own.

That is cheating!

Use Internet essays for research if credible (I'd be pretty leery of anything on the Internet that does not come from a credible website, and even some things from credible websites might have problems. Ask your professor). Look at an Internet essay's bibliography for additional sources, but that is it.

NEVER, EVER buy a paper on the Internet to turn in, or plagiarize from something on the Internet. That is cheating too, and professors know how to catch it.

IX
Presentations

"A lawyer friend of mine – a great guy, a
very smart guy – came up to me the other
day and said he heard that I had spoken
in front of 62,000 people in Los Angeles.
He said, 'How do you do that? Don't you
get scared?' I said, 'I don't want to think
about it.' It is true: I don't want to think
about it. I just do it. Then he called me up
the next day and said, 'That's the smartest
thing I've ever heard.'"—Donald Trump[30]

301. If you can walk and read, you can do a presentation.

Actually, you don't even need to walk. You can wheel yourself, or be wheeled or carried to the front of the class to give your presentation.

So many students are petrified of presentations, but every student who can read CAN do it. Students will have to give presentations at points in their college careers and in the working world, whether they like it or

---

[30] Donald J. Trump and Bill Zanker, *Think Big and Kick Ass in Business and Life* (New York: Collins, 2007), 62.

not. It is a valuable skill to be able to speak in front of others without passing out, crying or throwing up.

Everybody is nervous at first, even the most seasoned speaker. That nervousness and adrenalin keep one sharp and animated. The best talks and speeches come from animated speakers who excite the crowd. The worst type speaker is the sleeper with no adrenalin or animation, droning on and on.

Once one starts speaking, jitters begin to disappear and the speaker can even enjoy it! This is a fact. Seasoned speakers will confirm it. Some people become addicted to speaking in public. It's the adrenalin and recognition or a host of other reasons why, not the least of which is that other people can't do it. Speaking in public is an extremely valuable asset and a great thing to note on a resume.

A person speaking in front of a group never looks as nervous or bad as they think they do, and there are technical things a speaker can do to be more confident and deliver their talk easier.

302. If you have a choice, do a presentation on a topic that really interests you!

Treat a topic for a presentation the same as a topic for a paper. Pick something that excites you.

The more excited you are about your subject,

the more that excitement will come across when you speak. If you are bored with your subject, you will bore the class.

I did a presentation in a 300-level history course at the College of Charleston, *The Georgia/South Carolina/West Africa Connection*, under Dr. Alpha Bah. I did it on the Middle Passage, that trip on slave trading ships that poor captured Africans had to endure after being sold into slavery by other Africans in Africa, usually the result of tribal wars.

Tribal warfare and rivalry – Africans selling other Africans into slavery – were the basis of most African slavery because white people caught diseases on the African coast and usually did not disembark slave ships. They didn't need to. Black captives were already rounded up by tribal chieftains in places like Bunce Island, off the coast of modern Sierra Leone, waiting to be sold into slavery and carried all over the world. The forced exodus of so many Africans is called the African Diaspora.

Captives were chained to decks in the holds of burning hot ships that were like ovens with little ventilation, combining the stench of vomit, urine, feces and bodies chained next to each other the length and width of the ship for months at a time. It was said that one could smell a slave ship five miles away. This was the Middle Passage.

My purpose, with this topic, was to point out

that New Englanders were largely responsible for the Middle Passage because New England slave traders brought most of the slaves to America and made huge profits in the process.

I included in my talk several handouts with graphic drawings of the holds of New England slave trading ships. It showed a view as if the ship was sliced in half length-wise, so one could look at a side view of all the decks at once.

Africans were chained on their backs, packed in there side by side, on multiple decks. Many would die and not be removed for days. The stench and disease of the Middle Passage must have been unbelievable.

Half of the students in our class were white and half were black, and I had been a little leery of speaking so explicitly of the horrors of the Middle Passage to so many blacks, but my purpose was to expose New England guilt for inflicting the Middle Passage on hundreds of thousands of black Africans for profit and greed.

My presentation was successful and I was deeply touched when several black students came up to me personally and thanked me for not shying away from the horror of the Middle Passage but pointing it out explicitly. These fellow classmates were so sincere and appreciative, it really made me think about the intensity of emotion blacks have when studying slavery and the slave trade and how it evokes such powerful feelings for them today. This was eye-opening for me and made me a better historian and human being.

The point is, give your subject, or book on which you have to do an oral book report, some serious thought. Pick something that fires you up and don't shy away from anything.

Present the material in a factual and respectful manner, no matter what the subject. Use explicit drawings or reproductions of original documents and other graphical enhancements. Make it interesting.

Never pick a topic because it looks easy or because a lot of material is available. Your interest trumps ease. Do something different. Set yourself apart from the crowd. If your topic or book is fascinating to you, it will be just as fascinating to others, and your presentation will go well. You might really teach somebody something and you will make a higher grade.

303. Make sure you follow your professor's instructions to the letter. Always do this with any assignment.

For example, with an oral book report, you will probably have to turn in something written as well as give your presentation. Don't deviate one iota from your professor's instructions.

In fact, let me repeat: Throughout your college

career, make sure you understand your professor's instructions clearly, then follow them to the letter. This applies to every course and assignment. If you professor wants something a certain way and you give him/her something different, even if it is brilliant, you will lose points because you did not follow instructions. I can't stress this enough.

If you are presenting from your written book report, then make two copies. One, to turn in to your professor. The second, with oversize type, to present from.

304. Make the print much larger in the document or notes from which you will be presenting.

Make the text 20 or 30 points with one-and-a-half spaces between lines. Make it large enough to read easily at a glance. This trick will give you confidence.

Tag or highlight things you want to emphasize so they are easily recognizable as you present. Go so far as to highlight individual words on which you wish to place a greater emphasis or different inflection.

305. The days before your presentation, read out loud.

Reading out loud will also give you confidence. It strengthens your voice and improves articulation. It gives you poise.

Reading out loud on a regular basis at least once or twice a week, in the privacy of your home, is a great thing to do anyway.

As time gets closer to your presentation, read under conditions similar to how you must give your presentation. Stand up and look down at notes as if at a podium. Practice making eye contact with all parts of the room: left, center, right.

This practice will help you control nervousness and will give you confidence on presentation day, and you will make a better grade.

306. Speak with a strong voice. Don't be a shrinking violet or wimp.

Practice speaking with a strong, authoritative voice at home. If you do, speaking with a strong voice on presentation day will be a piece of cake. Do it. You don't have to yell, but you are giving a performance in front of a class and they will hate you if they can't hear you.

Well, they are your classmates. They won't hate you, but it will be uncomfortable for them and your professor. Have you ever been somewhere and the speaker was speaking so low you could barely hear him/her? Remember how aggravating it was?

Think about movie theaters. The sound is always loud enough, because a movie one could not hear would be a misery of straining and missed lines. It is loud enough so patrons don't have to strain.

Actors in plays know they must speak loud enough and with a strong enough voice to be heard easily by everybody in the audience. You are no different.

The act of speaking with a strong voice will get you going and make you confident as you deliver your talk. It will make your presentation a delight for your class even if they disagree with what you are saying.

307. Videotape yourself at home, or record your voice as you practice.

Look for ways to improve your delivery. Note strengths and weaknesses, and work on them. Develop a strong, confident, authoritative voice and tone.

308. Practice making eye contact with the class.

As you practice, look up and to the left, continue presenting, look up and in the center, continue presenting, look up and to the right. Repeat this, starting again from the left. Look at certain sympathetic people such as friends in different parts of the classroom.

At least make yourself look up every once in a while if you can't do it regularly. You will be so much more engaging and interesting to the class if you make eye contact with them at least once in a while.

One time I saw a gentleman with a doctorate deliver a paper to a scholarly conference and he did not look up a single time. He read the whole thing. He got through it, but he did not engage the crowd. He appeared amateurish and it took away from his paper. One would expect more composure from someone who has earned a doctorate.

If you practice looking up, you will be able to do it, at least some, on presentation day, especially if you start looking up early in your presentation.

309. Put your finger on your place in your notes as you look up at the class.

Your words will be oversize anyway, making them easy to read, so, keep your place with your finger as you look up at the class, then look down at your finger and quickly locate you place in your notes and continue on.

If you practice doing this at home, you will do it easily and naturally when you give your presentation.

310. Visualize yourself walking confidently up to the podium and giving a great presentation.

Use the trick of athletes and actors: Visualize! Imagine yourself walking up to the podium, starting with a strong voice and giving a great presentation after which your classmates jump out of their desks clapping loudly and give you a standing ovation!

Visualization is a powerful technique. When Rory McIlroy and Phil Mickelson think about the Masters, they are thinking about 25 foot putts rolling uphill on a slanted green curving down into the cup to the ecstasy of the crowd. They are not visualizing the ball lipping the cup to anguished "awhhhhhhh"s.

311. Visualization works for all human endeavors.

You can visualize success in your career, success in finding love, success on the athletic field, success giving presentations. In fact, all success is preceded by visualization.

So, visualize yourself dressed in your favorite clothes, walking up to the podium in front of your class with confidence, knowing your notes are highlighted, tagged and easy to read, knowing you are well-rehearsed and your voice is strong and articulate because you have been reading out loud for days, knowing you have practiced making eye-contact with your class, your vocal cords loose, and you don't have to pee. You are in great shape to give the performance of your life! Do it!

Then when it's over, pat yourself on the back because you deserve your "A".

312. On presentation day, wear clothes that make you confident, drink a little water to loosen vocal cords and go to the bathroom.

These are all tricks to give you confidence and help you with delivery. Everybody is nervous so don't focus on being nervous. Do like Donald Trump and don't think about it (or don't dwell on it), just get up and do it.

Be confident that you have good notes that are large enough to read easily, that you have been reading out loud for days so your voice is strong and articulate, that you are dressed in your favorite clothes and look great, and you are well-rehearsed. Then go kick some butt.

Also, remember. No matter what happens, the earth is not going to open up and swallow you nor will lightning come down and zap you. You are not going to have a heart attack or wet your pants.

Just rehearse ahead of time and you'll be amazed how easily things go. It will be a pleasure and make you proud.

313. Walk up to the podium with confidence. "Physicalize" the way actors do.

In addition to visualizing, actors also physicalize.

Actors know that stage fright is a real thing that must be controlled. One of their tricks is to get into action by physically moving on stage. Actors know that physical movement helps them focus on their parts and not their fright.

You do the same thing. When it's your turn, get up confidently and walk to the podium as if you are about to give an Academy Award Wining performance for which you are well prepared, then start with a strong voice. Once you start, you will be fine.

314. During your presentation, DO NOT EVER say you are nervous.

No matter how your presentation goes, never, ever, ever say you are nervous. It will not make you feel better to do so, and it will make you look amateurish and wimpy in front of the class.

Everybody is nervous. Even seasoned speakers are nervous. Ask classmates whose presentation went well if they were nervous, and they will tell you, HELL YES.

That type of nervousness is your friend. It keeps you focused and animated.

Just deliver your presentation as well as you

can. Don't think about yourself. I know that's
hard to do, but self-consciousness ruins
everything. Just do what you have to do, what you
have prepared yourself to do.

In fact, in life, don't be overly self-conscious.
Just be natural.

Get up there, do the best you can, thank the
class, then sit down.

**315. I watched a fellow give a good
presentation in a class then ruin it by saying that
he knew he was "boring" and couldn't continue.**

That was when I learned the lesson to NEVER
EVER EVER say you are nervous, boring, won't
do good, or any such negative talk. It will NOT
make you feel better or your presentation go
easier. You will be just as nervous but you'll have
tainted yourself and degraded your presentation
before even giving it, and it will translate into a
lower grade.

My friend from whom I learned this valuable
lesson had gone to the podium in front of a
History class of 30 students. He had started and
been fine, actually pretty good, certainly no worse
than anybody else. Then suddenly he said
something like, "I know I am boring and can't
continue," then his nervousness became obvious
and he sat down, looking foolish.

If he had simply said, "Hope y'all enjoyed it.

Thanks," then sat down, nobody would have known a thing! He would have looked so much better and gotten a better grade.

I saw a girl start crying during a presentation one time, and another girl quit. BOTH had been doing fine. Both came back later and finished, and both did as good as anybody else.

Don't psyche yourself out. Just prepare, then get up there and do it. Be yourself. Let your personality come out. Have fun.

316. Use transparencies or other visual aids to help with nervousness and to help cue you. Your talk will be more interesting.

Transparencies, handouts, pictures, video clips, notes on the board, and other visual aids are ways to greatly enhance your presentation and make it more interesting and understandable. Visual aids will also give you a great deal more confidence because you will know that they are there, like Linus's blanket, to whip out and impress your class. You will not have to face the class alone, as you would if you were just talking the whole time. You will have these fascinating visual aids to keep you on track and take the focus of the class off of you. Visual aids will help you speak better and move your presentation along.

Don't be afraid to use more than one visual aid. Use several, if appropriate. Use PowerPoint.

Your presentation is a creative endeavor, not unlike a performance in a play. Use whatever props will enrich that performance and help you deliver it.

Use everything you need, but nothing extra. Too many visual aids will weaken and water down your talk. Go for maximum impact. Sometimes less is more. Use your own judgment.

317. Use of visual aids will impress your professor.

It will appear, and rightly so, that you have done a lot more work for your presentation than the student who uses no visual aids.

So, not only do visual aids help you with nervousness and make your presentation more engaging and effective, you'll score higher with your professor! Use visual aids, the more interesting and apropos, the better!

318. If you can, go into your classroom before class and practice.

Stand up at the podium and see what it feels like to look out at your class. Practice looking to the left, center, right. Practice walking up to the podium from your usual desk.

Actually deliver your presentation quietly. Practice putting transparencies on the projector or turning on the DVD projector. Imagine yourself confident, composed, in control.

Be tough! Screw the class! Don't let it make you nervous. Be determined to give your talk as good as you can and to heck with whatever happens. As I've said, you won't be swallowed up by the earth, or zapped with a laser if you aren't quite up to Academy Award winning standards.

319. Make sure your notes and visual aids are in order.

You will be so much more confident if you can walk up to the podium and start without nervously fumbling for some chart or passage. Make sure you are organized. Practice at home so you know how to arrange your notes and visual aids, especially if you have something technical like video or audio to present.

320. Do a PowerPoint® presentation.

A PowerPoint presentation is very nice and effective if you are in an audio/video classroom with the necessary equipment. It will keep you on cue and provide a printout to hand out to the class so they can follow along.

If you are allowed to do a PowerPoint presentation, make sure you have a backup or two of the main file.

Also, make sure you get to class early and can

examine the computer and projection equipment to make sure it is operating. I have seen speakers go into panic after finding that the PowerPoint presentation on which they have spent so much time, is worthless, because equipment problems prevented them from showing it to the class.

Make sure you have a backup plan in case you have to ditch your PowerPoint presentation and talk from notes.

321. Don't chicken-out of doing a presentation. If you do, you will likely be penalized.

Usually you will be penalized for begging a professor to let you do something other than a presentation because you are too much of a wimp and too petrified to get up there with the rest of the class. You should be penalized. In life, you have to accept challenges and make things happen many times. Presentations are no different.

If you are overly nervous about a presentation – and I know a lot of students are, just like those who have a hard time asking and answering questions in class – then accept the presentation as a challenge. Use my tips and techniques. Practice at home. Overcome your nervousness. Learn how to win by dealing with uncomfortable things because there will be a ton of them in life coming fast your way. Make this attitude part of your life philosophy. Overcoming problems is the only way you get stronger and grow. Don't be a coward or wimp! Do your presentation with your class!

322. If you are also nervous about asking or answering questions in class MAKE yourself get over that too.

Do whatever it takes to learn to ask and answer questions in class. *Dare* yourself to answer one. Challenge yourself. Use my technique of answering the one-word questions. Build-up your confidence. It is highly desirable for a student to be able to participate in class, even on a limited basis. Do something! Don't just stare at the floor. Asking and answering questions in class and giving presentations with the rest of the class will build your confidence like nothing you can imagine and make you feel better about yourself and everything else in life.

No pain, no gain. The greater your fright, the prouder you will be for overcoming it, and the more confident and happy you will be. Make this a life philosophy.

X
Continue Strong
Winning, and the Philosophy of Success

"Winning is not everything. It is the only thing." – Vince Lombardi

"Whether you believe you can do a thing or believe you can't, you are right."
> – Henry Ford

"The longer I live, the more deeply I am convinced that that which makes the difference between one man and another – between the weak and the powerful, the great and the insignificant – is energy, invincible determination, a purpose once formed and then death or victory."
> – Fowell Buxton

"Success or failure in business is caused more by mental attitude even than by mental capacities." – Walter Dill Scott

"You can really have everything you want. If you go after it. But you will have to want it. The desire for success must be so strong within you that it is the very

*breath of your life — your first thought
when you awaken in the morning, your
last thought when you go to bed at night."*
                    – Charles E. Popplestone

*"The starting point of all achievement is
desire. Keep this constantly in mind.
Weak desires bring weak results, just as a
small amount of fire makes a small
amount of heat."* – Napoleon Hill

*"People do not lack strength; they lack
will."* – Victor Hugo

*"Success isn't a result of spontaneous
combustion. You must set yourself on
fire."* – Arnold H. Glasow

*"It's not the size of the man in the fight,
it's the size of the fight in the man."*
                    – Teddy Roosevelt

**323. Read about success and those who have
achieved it.**

You can develop a powerful attitude by
reading about success and those who have
achieved it. There is nothing so motivational as a
good story in which the hero bleeds and struggles
but refuses to be beaten, and finally wins. Be that

protagonist in your own story!

324. Accumulate a library of success books and refer back to them regularly.

The result of reading about success and successful people is the same as when you associate with successful people. Their success and good attitude rub off on you.

Once you go to an online book store such as Amazon.com, Alibris.com, AbeBooks.com, BarnesandNoble.com, BooksAMillion.com, et al., there are links to all the other success and positive mental attitude books. Many of them are also available as audio books.

Walk into a bookstore and look in the self-help and inspiration sections. In the bigger stores, there will be a *ton* of great books, old and new.

325. Buy the old classic, *Think and Grow Rich*, by Napoleon Hill.

Think and Grow Rich is the best selling success book of all time. Chapter 1, "The Power of Thought," starts with:

> TRULY, "thoughts are things," and powerful things at that, when they are mixed with definiteness of purpose, persistence and a BURNING DESIRE for their

translation into riches, or other
material objects.[31]

Need I say more.

And let me add "a BURNING DESIRE" for
not just "riches or material objects" but
intangibles such as graduating magna cum laude!
That was as tangible to me as the Atlantic Ocean,
and I had a BURNING DESIRE to get there and
was willing to sacrifice and work myself into the
ground, and I got there. So can you.

Napoleon Hill (1883-1970) wrote several other
outstanding books.

326. Buy *The Power of Positive Thinking*, by Norman Vincent Peale.

Dr. Norman Vincent Peale (1898-1993) is
another success author who has written numerous
books. One of his most famous is *The Power of
Positive Thinking*. Here's how it starts in Chapter
1, "Believe in Yourself":

BELIEVE IN YOURSELF! Have
faith in your abilities! Without a

---

[31] Napoleon Hill, *Think and Grow Rich* (1937; reprinted as
*Think and Grow Rich: The Landmark Bestseller-Now
Revised and Updated for the 21st Century;* rev. and
expanded by Arthur R. Pell—New York: Jeremy P.
Tarcher/Penguin, 2005), 1.

humble but reasonable confidence in
your own powers you cannot be
successful or happy. But with sound
self-confidence you can succeed. A
sense of inferiority and inadequacy
interferes with the attainment of
your hopes, but self-confidence leads
to self-realization and successful
achievement. Because of the
importance of this mental attitude,
this book will help you believe in
yourself and release your inner
powers.[32]

**327. Another classic is the huge 1936
bestseller, *How to Win Friends and Influence
People*, by Dale Carnegie.**

Dorothy Carnegie, wife of author Dale
Carnegie, writes this in the Preface to the 2009
reprint:

> *How to Win Friends and Influence
> People* was first published in 1937...
> took its place in publishing history as
> one of the all-time international best-
> sellers. It touched a nerve and filled
> a human need that was more than a
> faddish phenomenon of post-
> Depression days, as evidenced by its

---

[32] Norman Vincent Peale, *The Power of Positive Thinking*
(1952; reprint, New York: Ishi Press International, 2011), 1.

continued and uninterrupted
sales . . .[33]

This book has sold 15 million copies
worldwide. It remains popular today.

Dale Carnegie (1888-1955) wrote several other
success books.

**328. *The Art of War*, by Sun Tzu, edited by
James Clavell, is an enlightening book of
strategy and success.**

This great book was written 2,500 years ago
in China. Sun Tzu defines supreme excellence:

> To fight and conquer in all your
> battles is not supreme excellence;
> supreme excellence consists in
> breaking the enemy's resistance
> without fighting.[34]

Sun Tzu knew that planning is essential to
success on the battlefield.

> The general who wins a battle makes
> many calculations in his temple

---

[33] Dale Carnegie, *How to Win Friends and Influence People*,
(1936; reprint, New York: Simon & Schuster, 2009), Preface,
xi.

[34] Sun Tzu, *The Art of War*, James Clavell, ed. (New York:
Delacorte Press, 1983), 15.

before the battle is fought. The
general who loses a battle makes but
few calculations beforehand. Thus do
many calculations lead to victory,
and few calculations to defeat; how
much more no calculation at all![35]

329. Planning is also essential in life!

Planning leads to achievement of goals. Not
planning leads to floundering.

If you don't plan, you can't concentrate your
power or evaluate how you are doing. You can't
correct errors or stay on track.

Two millennium after Sun Tzu, and over a
century ago, French dramatist and writer, Victor
Hugo (1802-1885 – author of *The Hunchback of
Notre Dame*, and *Les Misérables*) echoed
Sun Tzu's sentiment:

He who every morning plans the
transactions of the day, and follows
out that plan, carries a thread that
will guide him through the labyrinth
of the most busy life. The orderly
arrangement of his time is like a ray
of light which darts itself through all
his occupations. But where no plan is
laid, where the disposal of time is
surrendered merely to the chance of

---

[35] Ibid., 11.

incidents, all things lie huddled
together in one chaos, which admits
of neither distribution nor review.[36]

**330. Read the autobiography of Wal-Mart
founder, Sam Walton.**

Sam's 1992 autobiography, *Made in America,
My Story*, by Sam Walton with John Huey, is a
powerhouse of inspiration that you will think
about every time you walk into Wal-Mart.

I have included some extra quotations here
because THIS is how you succeed in business.

> 'Wal-Mart is the finest-managed
> company we have ever followed. We
> think it is quite likely the finest-
> managed company in America, and
> we know of at least one investor who
> thinks it is the finest-managed
> company in the world. We do not
> expect to find another Wal-Mart in
> our lifetime . . .'—Margaret Gilliam,
> First Boston, around 1992[37]

---

[36] Victor Hugo quotation in *Elbert Hubbard's Scrap Book*
(New York: Wm. H. Wise & Co., Roycroft Distributors,
1923), 169.

[37] Sam Walton with John Huey, *Made in America, My Story*
(New York: Doubleday, 1992), 103.

'(Sam Walton) is the greatest businessman of this century.'—Harry Cunningham, Kmart Founder[38]

'I've known Sam since his first store in Newport, Arkansas, and I believe that money is, in some respects, almost immaterial to him. What motivates the man is the desire to absolutely be on top of the heap.'—Charlie Baum, Early Wal-Mart Partner[39]

Even when I was a little kid in Marshall, Missouri, I remember being ambitious. . . . I was so competitive that when I started Boy Scouts in Marshall I made a bet with the other guys about which one of us would be the first to reach the rank of Eagle. Before I made Eagle in Marshall, we had moved to the little town of Shelbina, Missouri – population maybe 1,500 – but I won the bet; I got my Eagle at age thirteen—the youngest Eagle Scout in the history of the state of Missouri at the time.[40]

---

[38] Ibid., 156.
[39] Ibid., 8.
[40] Ibid., 12.

'I remember him saying over and
over again: go in and check our
competition. Check everyone who is
our competition. And don't look for
the bad. Look for the good. If you get
one good idea, that's one more than
you went into the store with, and we
must try to incorporate it into our
company. We're really not concerned
with what they're doing wrong, we're
concerned with what they're doing
right, and everyone is doing
something right.'—Charlie Cate[41]

' (Sam Walton) is less afraid of being
wrong than anyone I've ever known.
And once he see he's wrong, he just
shakes it off and heads in another
direction.'—David Glass[42]

This is a big contradiction in my
makeup that I don't completely
understand to this day. In many of
my core values – things like church
and family and civic leadership and
even politics – I'm a pretty
conservative guy. But for some
reason in business, I have always
been driven to buck the system, to
innovate, to take things beyond

---

[41] Ibid., 63.
[42] Ibid., 39.

where they've been.[43]

I can tell you this, though: after a lifetime of swimming upstream, I am convinced that one of the real secrets to Wal-Mart's phenomenal success has been that very tendency. Many of our best opportunities were created out of necessity. The things that we were forced to learn and do, because we started out underfinanced and undercapitalized in these remote, small communities, contributed mightily to the way we've grown as a company.[44]

One way I've managed to keep up with everything on my plate is by coming in to the office really early almost every day, even when I don't have those Saturday numbers to look over. Four-thirty wouldn't be all that unusual a time for me to get started down at the office.[45]

'. . . If you take someone who lacks the experience and the know-how but has the real desire and the willingness to work his tail off to get the job done, he'll make up for what

---

[43] Ibid., 47.
[44] Ibid., 49.
[45] Ibid., 117.

he lacks. And that proved true nine times out of ten. It was one way we were able to grow so fast.'—Ferold Arend[46]

Around 1976 and 1977, we definitely got the message that Kmart – with 1,000 stores – thought Wal-Mart – with 150 – had gotten too big for its britches.... In 1976, we had a session of our discounters' trade group in Phoenix, and a lot of guys were talking about ways to avoid competing with Kmart directly. I got a little mad and told everybody they ought to stand up and fight them. I made it clear we planned to.[47]

If American business is going to prevail, and be competitive, we're going to have to get accustomed to the idea that business conditions change, and that survivors have to adapt to those changing conditions. Business is a competitive endeavor, and job security lasts only as long as the customer is satisfied. Nobody owes anybody else a living.[48]

---

[46] Ibid., 121.
[47] Ibid., 191-192.
[48] Ibid., 184.

This book is full of GOLD for entrepreneurs and people who plan business careers, especially in retail and marketing. There is a TON more extremely valuable information in this enjoyable book. It should be required reading for everybody in business.

331. Read some of Donald Trump's books.

I read *Think Big and Kick Ass, in Business and Life*, by The Donald, co-authored with Bill Zanker. This book is full of highly motivational material and excellent advice such as:

> To be a success the most important thing is to love what you do. You have to put in long hours and face enormous challenges to be successful. If you do not love what you do, you will never make it through. If you love your work, the difficulties will be balanced out by the enjoyment.[49]

> All successful people are high-energy people who are passionate about what they do. Find a passion that energizes you![50]

---

[49] Donald J. Trump and Bill Zanker, *Think Big and Kick Ass, in Business and Life* (New York: HarperCollins, 2007), 25.
[50] Ibid., 27.

Do not look for approval from others.
That is a sure sign of weakness.[51]

Some people carry around a lot of
mental baggage, which destroys their
focus. Get rid of it. It just gets in the
way and slows you down.[52]

The worse hell you will ever face is
the hell you create with your own
mind. It is much worse than the hell
other people create for you. So
instead of dwelling on all the
negatives, think about what you
want. Think about all the good
things you are going to do in life.
Keep focused on your goal and never
give up. Besides, bad times bring
great opportunities.[53]

**332. When you read an exceptionally
motivational quotation, look up the person saying
it and read a brief bio. Learn something about an
accomplished person.**

Just Google them and Wikipedia or
somewhere will pop up. It makes the quotation so
much more meaningful if you know a little about

---

[51] Ibid., 278.
[52] Ibid., 236.
[53] Ibid., 239.

the person saying it. You don't have to read much, just skim a few paragraphs and read what you want.

In the compilations below, there are hundreds of the most famous, accomplished men and women of all time whose stories and quotations are highly motivational.

One of them is Orison Swett Marden, founder of *Success* magazine and author of numerous books on success.

Also, Marden's original inspiration, Samuel Smiles. Smiles wrote hundreds of articles and twenty-five books including *Self-Help*, a best-selling classic celebrating achievement and self-reliance. It was published in 1859 but is still powerful reading and just as relevant today. The principles are the same.

333. Compilations of success quotations are jam-packed with crackling, buzzing electricity.

One can get lost in a bliss of quotations about success, determination, desire, discipline, achievement and the other things humans are geared to do.

These types of books show you the minds and raw drive of men and women determined to make things happen in their lives. They are the movers, shakers and achievers of the world, and will not be denied.

Compilations of success quotations can be read over and over throughout one's life for a shot of motivation or pure pleasure.

Here are a few I love:

"You know from past experience that whenever you have been driven to the wall, or thought you were, you have extricated yourself in a way which you never would have dreamed possible had you not been put to the test. The trouble is that in your everyday life you don't go deep enough to tap the divine mind within you."

— Orison Swett Marden

"Nothing in the world can take the place of persistence. Talent will not; nothing is more common than unsuccessful men with talent. Genius will not; unrewarded genius is almost a proverb. Education will not; the world is full of educated derelicts. Persistence and determination alone are omnipotent." – Calvin Coolidge

"You learn that, whatever you are doing in life, obstacles don't matter very much. Pain or other circumstances can be there, but if you want to do a job bad enough, you'll find a way to get it done." – Jack Youngblood

"This force, which is the best thing in you, your highest self, will never respond to any ordinary half-hearted call, or any milk-and-water endeavor. It can only be reached by your supremest call, your supremest effort. It will respond only to the call that is backed up by the whole of you, not part of you; you must be all there in what you are trying to do. You must bring every particle of your energy, unswervable resolution, your best efforts, your persistent industry to your task or the best will not come out of you. You must back up your ambition by your whole nature, by unbounded enthusiasm and a determination to win which knows no failure.... Only a masterly call, a masterly will, a supreme effort, intense and persistent application, can unlock the door to your inner treasure and release your highest powers." – Orison Swett Marden

"Get into a line that you will find to be a deep personal interest something you really enjoy spending twelve to fifteen hours a day working at, and the rest of the time thinking about."

– Earl Nightingale

"Success is not measured by what a man accomplished, but by the opposition he has encountered, and the courage with which he has maintained the struggle against overwhelming odds...." – Orison Swett Marden

"It is not ease, but effort — not facility, but difficulty, that makes men. There is, perhaps, no station in life in which difficulties have not to be encountered and overcome before any decided measure of success can be achieved."

— Samuel Smiles

"There are no gains without pains."

— Benjamin Franklin

"There is no success without hardship."

— Sophocles

"The measure of a man is the way he bears up under misfortune." — Plutarch

"The harder the conflict, the more glorious the triumph." — Thomas Paine

"No pain, no palm; no thorns, no throne; no gall, no glory; no cross, no crown." — William Penn

"People who have accomplished work worthwhile have had a very high sense of the way to do things. They have not been content with mediocrity. They have not confined themselves to the beaten tracks; they have never been satisfied to do things just as others do them, but always a little better. They always pushed things that came

to their hands a little higher up, a little farther. It is this little higher up, this little farther on, that counts in the quality of life's work. It is the constant effort to be first-class in everything one attempts that conquers the heights of excellence."
– Orison Swett Marden

"He that wrestles with us strengthens our nerves and sharpens our skill. Our antagonist is our helper." – Edmund Burke

"The very greatest things — great thoughts, discoveries, inventions — have usually been nurtured in hardship, often pondered in sorrow, and at length established with difficulty."
– Samuel Smiles

"First say to yourself what you would be; and then do what you have to do." – Epictetus

"This above all: to thine own self be true."
– William Shakespeare

"Know thyself." – Socrates

"You may have a fresh start any moment you choose, for this thing that we call 'failure' is not the falling down, but the staying down."
– Mary Pickford

"It's not over until it's over." – Yogi Berra

"What this power is I cannot say; all I know is that it exists and it becomes available only when a man is in that state of mind in which he knows exactly what he wants and is fully determined not to quit until he finds it." – Alexander Graham Bell

"If I had to select one quality, one personal characteristic that I regard as being most highly correlated with success, whatever the field, I would pick the trait of persistence. Determination. The will to endure to the end, to get knocked down seventy times and get up off the floor saying, 'Here goes number seventy-one!'"
    – Richard M. DeVos

"I do not think there is any other quality so essential to success of any kind as the quality of perseverance. It overcomes almost everything, even nature." – John D. Rockefeller

"Success... seems to be connected with action. Successful men keep moving. They make mistakes, but they don't quit." – Conrad Hilton

"'Where there is a will there is a way,' is an old and true saying. He who resolves upon doing a thing, by that very resolution, often scales the barriers to it, and secures its achievement. To think we are able, is almost to be so — to determine upon attainment is frequently attainment itself." – Samuel Smiles

"When your desires are strong enough you will appear to possess superhuman powers to achieve."
                                    – Napoleon Hill

"I have brought myself, by long meditation, to the conviction that a human being with a settled purpose must accomplish it, and that nothing can resist a will which will stake even existence upon its fulfillment." – Benjamin Disraeli

"There's a way to do it better... find it."
                                    – Thomas A. Edison

"It is not the critic who counts, not the man who points out where the strong stumbled, or how the doer could have done better. The credit belongs to the man who is actually in the arena; whose face is marred by dust and sweat and blood; who strives valiantly; who errs and comes short again and again; who knows the great enthusiasms, the great devotions, and spends himself in a worthy cause; who at the best knows in the end the triumph of high achievement; and who at the worst, if he fails, at least fails while daring greatly. His place shall never be with those cold and timid souls who know neither victory nor defeat." – Theodore Roosevelt

"The beginning of a habit is like an invisible thread, but every time we repeat the act we strengthen the strand, add to it another filament, until it becomes a great cable and binds us irrevocably thought and act."

– Orison Swett Marden

"The individual who wants to reach the top in business must appreciate the might of the force of habit — and must understand that practices are what create habits. He must be quick to break those habits that can break him — and hasten to adopt those practices that will become the habits that help him achieve the success he desires."

– J. Paul Getty

"Any act often repeated soon forms a habit; and habit allowed, steadily gains in strength. At first it may be but as a spider's web, easily broken through, but if not resisted it soon binds us with chains of steel." – Tryon Edwards

"I made a resolve then that I was going to amount to something if I could. And no hours, nor amount of labor, nor amount of money would deter me from giving the best that there was in me. And I have done that ever since, and I win by it. I know." – Colonel Harland Sanders

"All men who have achieved great things have been dreamers." – Orison Swett Marden

"Think little goals and expect little achievements. Think big goals and win big success." – David Joseph Schwartz

"We lift ourselves by our thought, we climb upon our vision of ourselves. If you want to enlarge your life, you must first enlarge your thought of it and of yourself. Hold the ideal of yourself as you long to be, always, everywhere — your ideal of what you long to attain — the ideal of health, efficiency, success."

– Orison Swett Marden

"Dream lofty dreams, and as you dream, so shall you become. Your vision is the promise of what you shall one day be; your ideal is the prophecy of what you shall at last unveil."

– James Allen

"Music should be something that makes you gotta move, inside or outside." – Elvis Presley

"Ambition is a dream with a V8 engine."

– Elvis Presley

334. The most powerful success material I ever read was compiled by American philosopher and writer, Elbert Hubbard, and published in 1923 with title *Elbert Hubbard's Scrap Book.*

I ran across *Elbert Hubbard's Scrap Book* when I was in my early 20s, the edition with copyright 1923 "By The Roycrofters" (published posthumously by William H. Wise & Company, Roycroft Distributors, New York City).

The title page states, almost as a subtitle:

> Containing the inspired and
> inspiring selections gathered during
> a lifetime of discriminating reading
> for his own use.

This 228 page book has subject, author and poetry indices, and is a product of the Arts and Crafts Movement of the early 20th century. It is ornate and decorative with hard brown covers tied together by cloth ribbon through three holes on the left-hand side.

335. *Elbert Hubbard's Scrap Book* is powerful.

Inside is some of the best writing and philosophy in the history of the world by people who lived from ancient times right up to

Hubbard's death in 1915.

The flavor of *Elbert Hubbard's Scrap Book* is definitely 19th century and before. Hubbard and his wife, Alice, died aboard the *RMS Lusitania* after it was torpedoed by the German submarine, *Unterseeboot 20*, on May 7, 1915 off the coast of Ireland two years before the United States entered World War I.

I read large parts of this book and found it so powerful and inspiring, it changed my life and has been a strong source of power and inspiration my entire life.

It also gave me a certain wisdom to have read the words of so many brilliant people across time.

336. Here are a few of the most powerful quotations for me from *Elbert Hubbard's Scrap Book*.

"No one has success until he has the abounding life. This is made up of the many-folded activity of energy, enthusiasm and gladness. It is to spring to meet the day with a thrill at being alive. It is to go forth to meet the morning in an ecstasy of joy. It is to realize the oneness of humanity in true spiritual sympathy."

– Lillian Whiting

"He who would do something great in this short life must apply himself to work with such a concentration of his forces as, to idle spectators who live only to amuse themselves, looks like insanity." – Francis Parkman, Jr.

"I never work better than when I am inspired by anger. When I am angry I can write, pray, and preach well; for then my whole temperament is quickened, my understanding sharpened, and all mundane vexations and temptations depart."

– Martin Luther

"Enthusiasm is the greatest asset in the world. It beats money and power and influence. Single-handed the enthusiast convinces and dominates where the wealth accumulated by a small army of workers would scarcely raise a tremor of interest. Enthusiasm tramples over prejudice and opposition, spurns inaction, storms the citadel of its object, and like an avalanche, overwhelms and engulfs all obstacles. It is nothing more or less than faith in action.

"Faith and initiative rightly combined remove mountainous barriers and achieve the unheard of and miraculous.

"Set the gem of enthusiasm afloat in your plant, in your office, or on your farm; carry it in your attitude and manner; it spreads like contagion and influences every fiber of your industry before you realize it; it means increase in production and decrease in costs; it means joy, and pleasure, and satisfaction to your workers; it means life, real, virile; it means spontaneous bedrock results – the vital things that pay dividends." – Henry Chester

"A great deal of talent is lost in the world for want of a little courage. Everyday sends to their graves obscure men whom timidity prevented from making a first effort; who, if they could have been induced to begin, would in all probability have gone great lengths in the career of fame. The fact is, that to do anything in the world worth doing, we must not stand back shivering and thinking of the cold and danger, but jump in and scramble through as well as we can. It will not do to be perpetually calculating risks and adjusting nice chances; it did very well before the Flood, when a man would consult his friends upon an intended publication for a hundred-and-fifty years, and live to see his success afterwards; but at present, a man waits, and doubts, and consults his brother, and his particular friends, till one day he finds he is sixty yeas old and that he has lost so much time in consulting cousins and friends that he has no more time to follow their advice."
                                        – Sydney Smith

"Oh, the eagerness and freshness of youth! How the boy enjoys his food, his sleep, his sports, his companions, his truant days! His life is an adventure, he is widening his outlook, he is extending his dominion, he is conquering his kingdom. How cheap are his pleasures, how ready his enthusiasms! In boyhood I have had more delight on a haymow with two companions and a big dog – delight that came nearer intoxication – than I have ever had in all the subsequent holidays of my life.

"When youth goes, much goes with it. When manhood comes, much comes with it. We exchange a world of delightful sensations and impressions for a world of duties and studies and meditations. The youth enjoys what the man tries to understand. Lucky is he who can get his grapes to market and keep the bloom under them, who can carry some of the freshness and eagerness and simplicity of youth into his later years, who can have a boy's heart below a man's head."

– John Burroughs

"Believe me when I tell you that thrift of time will repay you with a usury of profit beyond your most sanguine dreams; and that waste of it will make you dwindle alike in intellectual and moral stature, beyond your darkest reckoning."

– W. E. Gladstone

"If time be of all things most precious, wasting time must be the greatest prodigality, since lost time is never found again; and what we call time enough always proves little enough. Let us then be up and doing, and doing to a purpose; so by diligence shall we do more with less perplexity."

– Benjamin Franklin

"There are two ways of being happy: We may either diminish our wants or augment our means — either will do — the result is the same; and it is for each man to decide for himself, and do that which happens to be the easiest.

"If you are idle or sick or poor, however hard it may be to diminish your wants, it will be harder to augment your means.

"If you are active and prosperous or young or in good health, it may be easier to augment your means than to diminish your wants.

"But if you are wise, you will do both at the same time, young or old, rich or poor, sick or well; and if you are very wise you will do both in such a way as to augment the general happiness of society." – Benjamin Franklin

"The power of a man increases steadily by continuance in one direction. He becomes acquainted with the resistances and with his own tools; increases his skill and strength and learns the favorable moments and favorable accidents.

He is his own apprentice, and more time gives a great addition of power, just as a falling body acquires momentum with every foot of the fall."
                    – Ralph Waldo Emerson

"There is but one straight road to success, and that is merit. The man who is successful is the man who is useful. Capacity never lacks opportunity. It can not remain undiscovered, because it is sought by too many anxious to use it." – Bourke Cockran

"I never make the mistake of arguing with people for whose opinions I have no respect."
                    – Edward Gibbon

"If the world does owe you a living, you yourself must be your own collector."
                    – Theodore N. Vail

"He is not only idle who does nothing, but he is idle who might be better employed." – Socrates

"Every year I live I am more convinced that the waste of life lies in the love we have not given, the powers we have not used, the selfish prudence that will risk nothing, and which, shirking pain, misses happiness as well. No one ever yet was the poorer in the long run for having once in a lifetime

'let out all the length of all the reins.'"
– Mary Chalmondeley

"The law of worthy life is fundamentally the law of strife. It is only through labor and painful effort, by grim energy and resolute courage, that we move on to better things."
– Theodore Roosevelt

"Nature gives to every time and season some beauties of its own; and from morning to night, as from the cradle to the grave, is but a succession of changes so gentle and easy that we can scarcely mark their progress." – Charles Dickens

"Courage and perseverance have a magical talisman, before which difficulties disappear and obstacles vanish into air." – John Quincy Adams

"Self-confidence is the first requisite to great undertakings." – Samuel Johnson

"Habit is a cable; we weave a thread of it every day, and last we can not break it."
– Horace Mann

"Affection can withstand very severe storms of vigor, but not a long polar frost of indifference."
– Sir Walter Scott

"When one begins to turn in bed it is time to turn out." – Arthur Wellesley, 1st Duke of
Wellington

"Except a living man there is nothing more wonderful than a book! A message to us from the dead – from human souls we never saw, who lived, perhaps thousands of miles away. And yet these, in those little sheets of paper, speak to us, arouse us, terrify us, teach us, comfort us, open their hearts to us as brothers." – Charles Kingsley

"The men whom I have seen succeed best in life have always been cheerful and hopeful men, who went about their business with a smile on their faces, and took the changes and chances of this mortal life like men, facing rough and smooth alike as it came." – Charles Kingsley

"'Letting well enough alone' is a foolish motto in the life of a man who wants to get ahead. In the first place, nothing is 'well enough,' if you can do it better.

"No matter how well you are doing, do better. There is an old Spanish proverb which says, 'Enjoy the little you have while the fool is shunting for more.'

"The energetic American ought to turn this proverb upside down and make it read, 'While the fool is enjoying the little he has, I will hunt for more.'

"The way to hunt for more is to utilize your odd moments. Every minute that you save by making it useful, more profitable, is so much added to your life and its possibilities. Every minute lost is a neglected by-product — once gone, you will never get it back." – Arthur Brisbane

"Among the aimless, unsuccessful or worthless, you often hear talk about 'killing time.'

The man who is always killing time is really killing his own chances in life; while the man who is destined to success is the man who makes time live by making it useful." – Arthur Brisbane

"The ladder of life is full of splinters, but they always prick the hardest when we're sliding down." – William L. Brownell

"Forty is the old age of youth; fifty is the youth of old age." – Victor Hugo

"Fifty is the old age of youth; sixty is the youth of old age in 2012." – Gene Kizer, Jr.

"It is customary to say that age should be considered because it comes last. It seems just as much to the point that youth comes first. And the scale fairly kicks the beam if you go on to add that

age, in a majority of cases, never comes at all.
Disease and accidents make short work of even
the most prosperous persons. To be suddenly
snuffed out in the middle of ambitious schemes is
tragic enough at the best; but when a man has
been grudging himself his own life in the
meanwhile, and saving up everything for the
festival that was never to be, it becomes an
hysterically moving sort of tragedy which lies on
the confines of farce.... To husband a favorite
claret until the batch turns sour is not at all an
artful stroke of policy; and how much more with a
whole cellar – a whole bodily existence! People
may lay down their lives with cheerfulness in the
sure expectations of a blessed mortality; but that
is a different affair from giving up with all its
admirable pleasures, in the hope of a better
quality of gruel in a more than problematic, nay,
more than improbable old age. We should not
compliment a hungry man who should refuse a
whole dinner and reserve all this appetite for the
desert before he knew whether there was to be
any dessert or not. If there be such a thing as
imprudence in the world, we surely have it here.
We sail in leaky bottoms and on great and
perilous waters; and to take a cue from the
dolorous old naval ballad, we have heard the
mermaids singing, and know that we shall never
see dry land any more. Old and young, we are all

on our last cruise. If there is a fill of tobacco
among the crew, for God's sake, pass it round and
let us have a pipe before we go!"

– Robert Louis Stevenson

"You want a better portion than you now have
in business, a better and fuller place in life. All
right, think of that better place and you in it.
Form the mental image. Keep on thinking of that
higher position, keep the image constantly before
you, and – no, you will not suddenly be
transported into the higher job, but you will find
that you are preparing yourself to occupy the
better position in life – your body, your energy,
your understanding, your heart will all grow up to
the job – and when you are ready, after hard
work, after perhaps years of preparation, you will
get the job and the higher place in life."

– Joseph H. Appel

"Why should we call ourselves men, unless it
is to succeed in everything, everywhere? Say of
nothing, 'This is beneath me,' nor feel that
anything is beyond our powers. Nothing is
impossible to the man who can will."

– Honoré Mirabeau

"The man who starts out with the idea of
getting rich won't succeed; you must have a larger
ambition. There is no mystery in business success.

If you do each day's task successfully, stay
faithfully within the natural operations of
commercial law, and keep your head clear, you
will come out all right." – John D. Rockefeller

"I owe all my success in life to having been
always a quarter of an hour beforehand."
                            – Horatio Lord Nelson

"The men who try to do something and fail are
infinitely better than those who try to do nothing
and succeed." – Lloyd Jones

"To love and win is the best thing; to love and
lose the next best."
                        – William Makepeace Thackeray

Playthings
By Robert Louis Stevenson

The streets are full of human toys,
Wound up for threescore years;
Their springs are hungers, hopes and joys,
And jealousies and fears.

They move their eyes, their lips, their Hands;
They are marvelously dressed;
And here my body stirs or stands,
A plaything like the rest.

The toys are played with till they fall,
Worn out and thrown away.
Why were they ever made at all!
Who sits to watch that play!

337. Other quotations by Elbert Hubbard himself.

"There is no failure except in no longer trying. There is no defeat except from within, no really insurmountable barrier save our own inherent weakness of purpose."

"At last we must admit that the man who towers above his fellows is the one who has the power to make others work for him; a great success is not possible any other way."

"To remain on earth you must be useful. Otherwise, Nature regards you as old metal and is only watching for a chance to melt you over."

"Genius may have its limitations, but stupidity is not thus handicapped."

"Life is just one damned thing after another."

"To avoid criticism do nothing, say nothing, be nothing."

"The greatest mistake you can make in life is to be continually fearing you will make one."

"One machine can do the work of fifty ordinary men. No machine can do the work of one extraordinary man."

"You can lead a boy to college, but you can't make him think."

"We awaken in others the same attitude of mind we hold toward them."

"The love we give away is the only love we keep."

"Prison is a Socialist's Paradise, where equality prevails, everything is supplied and competition is eliminated."

"Do not take life too seriously. You will never get out of it alive."

338. Find and clip stirring words anywhere, and make them yours.

This was an ad in the *Wall Street Journal*, December 5, 1985 sponsored by United Technologies of Hartford, Connecticut. At the bottom, it read "How we perform as individuals will determine how we perform as a nation."

To the Kid on the End of the Bench

Champions once sat where you're sitting, kid. The Football Hall of Fame (and every other Hall of Fame) is filled with names of people who sat, week after week, without getting a spot of mud on their well-laundered uniforms. Generals, senators, surgeons, prize-winning novelists, professors, business executives started on the end of a bench, too. Don't sit and study your shoe tops. Keep your eye on the game. Watch for defensive lapses. Look for offensive opportunities. If you don't think you're in a great spot, wait until you see how many would like to take it away from you at next spring practice. What you do from the bench this season could put you on the field next season as a player, or back in the grandstand as a spectator.

339. There are excellent success-quotation websites on the Internet. Search for "success quotations."

The great thing about quotation websites is the vast amount of information, all cataloged by author and subject. Do a Google search for "success quotations" or "famous quotations" and all kinds of things will pop up.

A good website is The Quotations Page at www.quotationspage.com. Their home page boasts that it is the oldest quotation website, established in 1994, and today (March, 2013) has 27,000 quotations from 3,100 authors with more added daily.[54] There are extensive quotations, from Aristotle to Elizabeth Clarkson Zwart. It's a philosophical feast! And all are categorized by author and subject. Here are three:

"Security is mostly a superstition. It does not exist in nature .... Life is either a daring adventure or nothing." – Helen Keller

"Duty then is the sublimest word in the English language. You should do your duty in all things. You can never do more, you should never wish to do less." – Gen. Robert E. Lee

"How far you go in life depends on your being tender with the young, compassionate with the aged, sympathetic with the striving, and tolerant of the weak and the strong. Because someday in

---

[54] The Quotations Page, http://www.quotationspage.com, accessed March 28, 2013.

life you will have been all of these."

– George Washington Carver

340. Another good website is www.BrainyQuote.com.[55] **Here are a few from H. L. Mencken**

> **Henry Louis "H. L." Mencken**
> (September 12, 1880 – January 29, 1956), the "Sage of Baltimore," was one of the most influential American writers of the twentieth century, a journalist, editor, satirist and critic of American culture. Several of his books are still in print.

"An idealist is one who, on noticing that roses smell better than a cabbage, concludes that they will also make better soup."

"Immorality: the morality of those who are having a better time."

"It is impossible to imagine the universe run by a wise, just and omnipotent God, but it is quite easy to imagine it run by a board of gods."

"No married man is genuinely happy if he has to drink worse whiskey than he used to drink

---

[55] BrainyQuote, http://www.BrainyQuote.com, accessed March 28, 2013.

when he was single."

"No matter how happily a woman may be married, it always pleases her to discover that there is a nice man who wishes that she were not."

"Puritanism. The haunting fear that someone, somewhere, may be happy."

"The theory seems to be that as long as a man is a failure he is one of God's children, but that as soon as he succeeds he is taken over by the Devil."

341. More from www.BrainyQuote.com:

Here's one from the guy who wrote *God Bless America*:

> **Irving Berlin**, May 11, 1888- September 22, 1989, was a brilliant American composer and songwriter who wrote *God Bless America, White Christmas, There's No Business Like Show Business*, and many other great songs.

"Our attitudes control our lives. Attitudes are a secret power working twenty-four hours a day, for good or bad. It is of paramount importance that we know how to harness and control this great force." – Irving Berlin

"I honestly think it is better to be a failure at something you love than to be a success at something you hate." – George Burns

"Success is to be measured not so much by the position that one has reached in life as by the obstacles which he has overcome."
            – Booker T. Washington

"Excellence is to do a common thing in an uncommon way." – Booker T. Washington

"Action is the foundational key to all success."
            – Pablo Picasso

"Don't aim for success if you want it; just do what you love and believe in, and it will come naturally." – David Frost

"Each player must accept the cards life deals him or her; but once they are in hand, he or she alone must decide how to play the cards in order to win the game." – Voltaire

"No problem can withstand the assault of sustained thinking." – Voltaire

"Excellence is an art won by training and habituation. We do not act rightly because we have virtue or excellence, but we rather have those because we have acted rightly. We are what we repeatedly do. Excellence, then, is not an act but a habit." – Aristotle

"I count him braver who overcomes his desires than him who conquers his enemies; for the hardest victory is over self." – Aristotle

"Men acquire a particular quality by constantly acting in a particular way." – Aristotle

"Moral excellence comes about as a result of habit. We become just, by doing just acts, temperate by doing temperate acts, brave by doing brave acts." – Aristotle

"The aim of art is to represent not the outward appearance of things, but their inward significance." – Aristotle

"You will never do anything in this world without courage. It is the greatest quality of the mind next to honor." – Aristotle

"Youth is easily deceived because it is quick to hope." – Aristotle

"Love begets love, love knows no rules, this is same for all." – Virgil

"Love conquers all." – Virgil

"Love conquers all things; let us too surrender to Love." – Virgil

"When I don't know whether to fight or not, I always fight." – Horatio Lord Nelson

"All the world's a stage, and all the men and women merely players: they have their exits and their entrances; and one man in his time plays many parts, his acts being seven ages."
– William Shakespeare, from *As You Like It*,
Act II, Scene VII

"Cowards die many times before their deaths; the valiant never taste of death but once."
– William Shakespeare, from *Julius Caesar*,
Act II, Scene II

"Life's but a walking shadow, a poor player, that struts and frets his hour upon the stage, and then is heard no more; it is a tale told by an idiot, full of sound and fury, signifying nothing."
– William Shakespeare, from *Macbeth*,
Act V, Scene V

"Nothing is really good or bad in itself – it's all what a person thinks about it."
                              – William Shakespeare, from *Hamlet,*
                                                  Act II, Scene II

"This above all: to thine own self be true, and it must follow, as the night the day, thou canst not then be false to any man."
                              – William Shakespeare, from *Hamlet,*
                                                  Act I, Scene III

"Courage is the greatest of all virtues, because if you haven't courage, you may not have an opportunity to use any of the others."
                                             – Samuel Johnson

"If your determination is fixed, I do not counsel you to despair. Few things are impossible to diligence and skill. Great works are performed not by strength, but perseverance."
                                             – Samuel Johnson

"Self-confidence is the first requisite to great undertakings." – Samuel Johnson

"So far is it from being true that men are naturally equal, that no two people can be half an hour together, but one shall acquire an evident superiority over the other." – Samuel Johnson

"The chains of habit are too weak to be felt until they are too strong to be broken."

— Samuel Johnson

"The greatest part of a writer's time is spent in reading in order to write. A man will turn over half a library to make a book." — Samuel Johnson

"There is no private house in which people can enjoy themselves so well as at a capital tavern .... No, Sir; there is nothing which has yet been contrived by man by which so much happiness is produced as by a good tavern or inn."

— Samuel Johnson

"Beer is living proof that God loves us and wants us to be happy." — Benjamin Franklin

"Energy and persistence conquer all things."

— Benjamin Franklin

"Speak ill of no man, but speak all the good you know of everybody." — Benjamin Franklin

"Take time for all things: great haste makes great waste." — Benjamin Franklin

"Tell me and I forget. Teach me and I remember. Involve me and I learn."

— Benjamin Franklin

"One ought never to turn one's back on a threatened danger and try to run away from it. If you do that, you will double the danger. But if you meet it promptly and without flinching, you will reduce the danger by half. Never run away from anything. Never!" – Winston Churchill

342. Know Vince Lombardi, immortal coach of the Green Bay Packers.

Coach Lombardi won numerous championships including the first two Super Bowls for the 1966 and '67 seasons. He never had a losing season in the NFL. He is the epitome of drive, determination, blood, sweat and achievement.

What It Takes to be Number One

From the Lombardi web site,
www.VinceLombardi.com

Winning is not a sometime thing; it's an all the time thing. You don't win once in a while; you don't do things right once in a while; you do them right all the time. Winning is a habit. Unfortunately, so is losing.

There is no room for second place. There is only one place in my game, and that's first place. I have finished second twice in my time at Green Bay, and I don't ever want to finish second again. There is a second place bowl game, but it is a game for losers played by losers. It is and always has been an American zeal to be first in anything we do, and to win, and to win, and to win.

Every time a football player goes to play his trade he's got to play from the ground up – from the soles of his feet right up to his head. Every inch of him has to play. Some guys play with their heads. That's O.K. You've got to be smart to be number one in any business. But more importantly, you've got to play with your heart, with every fiber of your body. If you're lucky enough to find a guy with a lot of head and a lot of heart, he's never going to come off the field second.

Running a football team is no different than running any other kind of organization – an army, a political party or a business. The principles are the same. The object is to win – to beat the other guy. Maybe that sounds hard or cruel. I don't think it is.

It is a reality of life that men are competitive and the most competitive games draw the most competitive men. That's why they are there – to compete. To know the rules and objectives when they get in the game. The object is to win fairly, squarely, by the rules – but to win.

And in truth, I've never known a
man worth his salt who in the long run,
deep down in his heart, didn't appreciate
the grind, the discipline. There is
something in good men that really
yearns for discipline and the harsh
reality of head to head combat.

I don't say these things because I
believe in the 'brute' nature of man or
that men must be brutalized to be
combative. I believe in God, and I believe
in human decency. But I firmly believe
that any man's finest hour – his greatest
fulfillment to all he holds dear – is that
moment when he has to work his heart
out in a good cause and he's exhausted
on the field of battle – victorious.

—Coach Vince Lombardi[56]

**343. Other quotations by Vince Lombardi,
also on the website.**

"Dictionary is the only place that success
comes before work. Hard work is the price we
must pay for success. I think you can accomplish
anything if you're willing to pay the price."

---

[56] Vince Lombardi, "What It Takes to be Number One",
http://www.vincelombardi.com/number-one.html, accessed
March 28, 2013.

"Winning is habit. Unfortunately, so is losing."

"The harder you work, the harder it is to surrender."

"Teams do not go physically flat, but they go mentally stale."

"Fatigue makes cowards of us all."

344. Powerful statements about Vince Lombardi by some of his players, from the book *Lombardi, Winning Is the Only Thing*, edited by Jerry Kramer. [57]

Jerry Kramer played at Green Bay for 11 years as an offensive lineman. During that time, the Packers won five National Championships and the first two Super Bowls. He's most famous for the 1967 NFL Championship Game known as the Ice Bowl played against the Dallas Cowboys at Green Bay in sub-zero temperatures.

The Packers were down 17-14 with 16 seconds left in the game. It was third and goal from the two-foot line. If they ran and didn't score, the clock would run out and they would lose. The smarter play was a pass, so that if incomplete it would stop the clock and give them enough time

---

[57] Jerry Kramer, ed., *Winning Is the Only Thing* (New York: The World Publishing Company, 1970).

to set up for the tying field goal to go into overtime.

Kramer assured Quarterback Bart Starr he could block on the frozen ground so Starr called a right 31 wedge with himself keeping.

On the snap, Kramer and center Ken Bowman instantly executed a perfect double-team block on the Cowboy's Jethro Pugh and Starr got across the goal line! The Packers had won one of the greatest NFL games in history, 21-17.

Kramer is in the Green Bay Hall of Fame and his jersey retired. He is the author of several books including the best-selling *Instant Replay*, with Dick Schaap. He was also a sports commentator.

Alex Wojciechowicz[58]

Vince went into every game with the
attitude, 'I'm here to die, are you?'
He was ready to kill himself to win.
He never said much. He was a leader
by example. One game, someone hit
him in the mouth, and he played the
whole sixty minutes, cut and

---

[58] Wojciechowicz played on the offensive line at Fordham University in 1936 and '37 with Lombardi when Fordham was a football powerhouse. He and Lombardi were two of the famed Seven Blocks of Granite. Wojciechowicz went on to become an NFL Hall of Famer.

bleeding, then went and got about
twenty stitches in his mouth.

Bart Starr[59]

I wasn't mentally tough before I met
Coach Lombardi. . . . To win, you
have to have a certain amount of
mental toughness. Coach Lombardi
gave me that. He taught me that you
must have a burning desire to win.
It's got to dominate all your waking
hours. It can't ever wane. It's got to
glow in you all the time.

. . . And in 1960, when we had to beat
Los Angeles in the final game of the
season to clinch the conference title, I
was really ill. I got violently sick to
my stomach during the game. But I
kept playing—I was mentally tough;
I wouldn't give in to my sickness—
and we won the game.

I wanted to be one of the best
quarterbacks in pro football, and I

[59] Starr was the Green Bay Packers' famed quarterback
from 1956 to 1971, winning several NFL championships and
the first two Super Bowls in which he was MVP in both. He
is another Pro Football Hall of Famer and is also in the
Green Bay Packers Hall of Fame. He played college football
at Alabama. He had an NFL playoff record of 9-1, and the
NFL's best passing completion percentage (57.4) when he
retired in 1972.

knew I didn't have the strongest arm
in the world. I knew I wasn't the
biggest guy or the fastest. But Coach
Lombardi showed me that, by
working hard and using my mind, I
could overcome my weaknesses to
the point where I could be one of the
best.

The heart of his system was
preparation. He prepared us
beautifully for every game, and for
every eventuality. That—more than
the words of encouragement he
occasionally gave me—was what
built up my self-confidence. Thanks
to Coach Lombardi, I knew—I was
positive—that I would never face a
situation I wasn't equipt to handle.

Paul Hornung[60]

I don't believe any team went into its
game each Sunday as well prepared

---

[60] Hornung is a Heisman Trophy winner and was inducted
into both the Pro Football Hall of Fame and College
Football Hall of Fame. He played at Notre Dame and was
the number one draft pick in 1957, taken by the Green Bay
Packers. Hornung played for Lombardi for eight years and
became a star, breaking scoring records, many of which still
stand. In 1960, he scored 176 points in a 12-game season.
Green Bay won four league championships in those days
including the first Super Bowl in 1967.

as we were. We knew just what to
expect.

For instance, if we were playing
the Baltimore Colts and we had the
ball on the left side of the field
between the forty-yard lines, we
knew that, on third down, the Colts
would throw up a zone defense
against us. And we knew exactly how
to attack that zone. The quarterback
knew which plays to call, and the
linemen knew how to adjust. Every
single one of our linemen knew what
a zone was. Hell, before Vince got
there, even our quarterbacks—I was
one of them—didn't know what a
zone was. We just called some kind of
pass on third down, and that was it.
If it went incomplete, we just figured
it was a bad pass. Vince made us the
smartest team in football.

Frank Gifford[61]

I can remember sneaking out some

---

[61] Gifford was an All-American at the University of
Southern California in 1951 and '52, and is another Pro
Football Hall of Famer. He spent 12 seasons with the NY
Giants, and five of those were under head coach Vince
Lombardi before Lombardi's Green Bay days. In each of
Gifford's seasons under Lombardi, he was nominated for the
Pro Bowl, and they never had a losing record. After football,
Gifford became a sportscaster. He is married to Kathie Lee
Gifford.

nights after curfew in Oregon, and
sometimes I'd come back in pretty
late, and the lights would still be on
in his room. I realized then the kind
of work he was putting in. He had to
be exhausted, but he never showed
it. He'd be out on the field the next
day, going full speed, driving himself
every minute.

Vinny believes in the Spartan life,
the total self-sacrifice, and to succeed
and reach the pinnacle that he has,
you've got to be that way. You've got
to have total dedication. The hours
you put in on a job can't even be
considered. The job is to be done . . . I
saw the movie, Patton, and it was
Vince Lombardi.

Sam Huff[62]

I love football, I love the game more
than anything in the world, but my

---

[62] Huff was inducted into the NFL Hall of Fame in 1982. He
played middle linebacker for the NY Giants from 1956 to
'63, and for six of those years, the Giants won the division
title. For four of those years, Huff was All-Pro. He spent
four years with the Washington Redskins then retired
before Lombardi talked him out of retirement. He became a
player/coach for the Redskins under Lombardi in 1969, and
they went 7-5-2. That kept Lombardi's record of never
coaching a losing NFL team, intact.

dedication equals one-third of his.
It's his life. I remember one time we
were watching some films, Kansas
City versus Green Bay in the Super
Bowl. On one play, Jimmy Taylor
took off through tackle and broke to
the outside and went for the
touchdown. I think he carried about
three guys with him. Lombardi,
watching, was up and screaming,
'Look at that sonuvabitch run!' I
guarantee he'd seen that film two
hundred times, but he couldn't
contain his enthusiasm.

Norb Hecker[63]

Of course, Vince admired great
speakers. He had a record of Gen.
MacArthur's famous speech to the
cadets at West Point, the one about
love, honor and duty, and he used to
play that record over and over in the
coaches' room. You got tears in your
eyes listening to it; it was fantastic.

---

[63] Hecker was an assistant coach under Vince Lombardi in
Green Bay from 1959 to '65. In his career, he was a part of
eight NFL championship teams and was the first head
coach of the Atlanta Falcons.

345. If you draw power from other sources such as your faith or family, then nurture them too. Nurture all sources of power.

Put a lot into whatever gives you power! You can't get more out than you put in. Put a lot in! Especially if your effort is multiplied.

Don't listen to what anybody else says. Follow your heart. It's YOUR life and it's shorter than you think. Know yourself, as Socrates said. To thine own self be true, as Shakespeare said. Go after everything you want! Play the game with heart from the bottoms of your feet to the top of your head, as Lombardi said!

Having a philosophy of success in your mind will unleash a power you never knew you had. It is something that stays with you, something you can rely on to be there for you always! Nurture it! Promote it. You will be happy and fulfilled doing so.

346. Do things that give you confidence. I ran four marathons!

I ran 26.2 mile races four times—the **Island Marathon** (Isle of Palms, SC early 1980s, my best time: 3 hrs., 23 mins.), the **Savannah Marathon**, the **Marine Corps Marathon**, and the **Shut-In Ridge Run** (I count this as a marathon because it was more grueling—17 miles up Little Pisgah!).

My marathons were difficult goals and I went after them with a vengeance. I also ran over fifty 10Ks and races of other distances. I had a blast doing so.

I think back on those days and it gives me a good feeling to know I had the guts to take on huge challenges and was man enough to make them happen. I will always feel great about my marathons and NOBODY can take them away from me.

347. I was determined to graduate magna cum laude, one of the greatest goals of my life.

And in the process, I ended up achieving History Departmental Honors and the Outstanding Student Award for the History Department, as well the Rebecca Motte American History Award the year before.

I was determined and was not going to be denied. I was willing to do whatever it took, and that meant long, long hours and TOTAL commitment.

I achieved my goals and those victories are mine to savor forever.

348. And now my goal is to help YOU do it!

Just imagine how good graduating magna cum laude will make you feel! Not to mention

what you'll learn! And you'll feel that way the rest
of your life. It's like winning an Olympic Gold
Medal!

Of course if you've been playing too hard, just
graduating, PERIOD, will make you feel pretty
damn good too!

349. Do things that discourage self-consciousness.

Self-consciousness diverts focus in a critical
way from your goals to your self. Don't paralyze
yourself with self-consciousness. It ruins
everything and is a waste of time.

Take on things that scare you! Jump out of a
plane. Run a marathon. Anything that you know
is a weakness, attack it. Even if you attack in a
small way. Put yourself on the road to overcoming
all problems, especially shyness and things that
make you self-conscious.

Keep yourself positive. Keep your goals before
you. Whatever is causing you to be self-conscious
or ineffective, defeat it! You have the power. Use
it.

350. Keep your body strong and fit.

It's hard to have a mind like a steel-trap if
your body is flab. Shape up! Walk, run, bike ride.
Go to the gym. Lift weights. Swim. Be physical.

You will not believe how much better you look and feel, and how much more you will enjoy life.

351. America is a land of unlimited opportunity.

> It is and always has been an American zeal to be first in anything we do, and to win, and to win, and to win.—Vince Lombardi

Decide what you want then GO GET IT! There is nothing in your way except your own self.

You've only got one life and it's short, though it might not seem short.

I know it is hard for young people to see far into the future. Y'all have an immortality mindset just like the old man and old woman walking down the street once had.

And that's fine. It's normal. It's human.

The way for young people to go into the future as if you have a road map is first pursue what you love! Pursue the things that stimulate and motivate you, and pursue them HARD and with great vigor.

Then, just stay on track. Do things that help you such as more education, more experiences, staying in shape, eating healthy, being happy, having fun. Make *sure* you don't get hooked on anything like cigarettes, drugs, gambling . . . anything that controls you instead of *you* controlling it!

If your interests change, pursue your new interest with just as much energy. I know people who graduated from law school then decided they didn't want to practice law and got into other fields.

I know people in other fields who decided they wanted to go to law school at middle age and did that.

I know people who have become writers at all ages, and LOTS of people who have started businesses at all ages!

There is simply no limit in America. Give back to your country and make sure it stays a land of individual freedom and responsibility, and unlimited opportunity!

Go have a GREAT life! I hope I have added to it.

— Gene

Index

*of All 351 Bold Topic Sections
by Chapter*

I
Start Strong
Be Organized and in Control

1. Buy an inexpensive desk calendar.

2. Go further. Put down the dates on which you need to begin each assignment.

3. Another reason to know everything that is coming up: Fear of the unknown.

4. If you don't take control of your coursework and schedule, you are blowing in the wind.

5. Make SURE you understand how much everything counts toward your grade.

6. Note whether you can earn extra credit.

7. Make sure you buy ALL your school books for the semester, the sooner the better.

8. Make sure you have a dictionary, thesaurus and other personal reference books unique to your field.

9. It's good to have a desktop encyclopedia, though a Google search of any topic will usually turn up several good sources such as Wikipedia.

10. During the semester, CliffsNotes®, SparkNotes® or an equivalent study guide WILL come in handy.

11. Many study guides are not just literary.

12. You might want to create your own study aid in a course by copying the glossary or other material in the back of a book.

13. Include, as one of your reference books, *The Elements of Style* by William Strunk, Jr. and E. B. White.

14. Writing is a critical skill for ALL students and for people in the workforce. Read E. B. White's essay on writing in *The Elements of Style*: "An Approach to Style (With a List of Reminders)." It is outstanding!

15. Two other EXCELLENT books on writing will help you enormously.

16. An excerpt from Stephen King's *On Writing*.

17. Short excerpts from William Zinsser's *On Writing Well*.

18. Use only notebooks with a pocket in the front. One-subject notebooks are best.

19. Make sure somebody can find you to return a lost notebook.

20. Put all of your school materials in one place in your room or house.

21. Find your college library and other libraries in your area that you can use.

22. Libraries are EXTREMELY valuable assets.

23. Walk into a library and feel the power, knowledge, art, culture, history, literature, and science stored there.

24. Don't hesitate to ask a reference librarian a question, or use interlibrary loan.

25. When you go to the stacks to look for a book, remember, there are likely several other books around that book on the same topic.

26. Always carry change and some dollars in your backpack in case you need to make copies.

27. Make copies of *every* article you are supposed to read, so you own them.

28. Do all your copying for the semester at one time, if possible.

29. If you can't do a whole semester's worth of copying and downloading, then do half the semester.

30. Whatever you do, don't wait until the last minute to make copies or read something.

31. You need a computer with Internet access, and a printer.

32. Electrical surge protection and virus protection for your computer are critical.

33. If a course has material on the Internet, bookmark the website early on.

34. Create a master directory (folder) on your computer for the semester. Here's what to do using Windows *(Apple people please follow same procedures using Apple protocol).*

35. Create folders INSIDE your master folder for your individual courses.

36. Create additional folders inside your course folders if you want to.

37. You don't have to put your master folder in Documents.

38. If you want your master folder to appear first, in Documents, or earlier than its alphabetization would allow, then simply put a 0 or 1 in front of the folder name.

39. You can change the name of any folder or file at any time, easily.

40. Download everything for the semester at one time, if possible.

41. Save your downloaded files in the appropriate course folder.

42. Here's a link to some good information on files and folders from Microsoft. I'm sure Apple has similar information easily accessible.

43. Make a backup copy of your master folder on a flash drive.

44. It's easy to make a copy of your master folder.

45. Always create TWO files of anything you are working on in case you accidentally delete the main one, or the main one becomes corrupted. Here's an easy way to do it.

46. Save individual files you are working on to both your master folder AND the master folder backup on your flash drive.

47. Also back up your work to a CD or DVD, something that is separate from your computer in case your computer blows up.

48. Consider subscribing to a service that backs up your files automatically.

49. BE EXTREMELY CAREFUL when copying files and folders. You can destroy all your work if you aren't.

50. A deleted file will stay in your Recycle Bin until you use the "Empty the Recycle Bin" command.

51. All of the above ideas for backing up files and folders are outstanding, but develop your own.

52. It's a good idea to print, every so often, a paper or other assignment you are working on.

II
Professors

53. Professors are people too!

54. Do some research on your professors.

55. You might be impressed with your professors' accomplishments.

56. One day you might need letters of recommendation for graduate school or for scholarships and grants, or you might need references in the working world.

57. Grading is subjective, especially on essay and discussion exams, so think about this.

58. Though professors are people too, always use your head.

59. Not all professors are good professors.

60. Academia is clearly liberal. Over 80% of professors are liberals and most are Democrats. It is an indisputable fact of college life.

61. More than likely, a professor's liberal ideology is not going to be a problem because professors know there are twice as many conservatives in the county as liberals.

62. Liberal bias sneaks in constantly, so be aware.

63. "Word of mouth" about professors: take it with a grain of salt.

64. Definitely use RateMyProfessors.com.

65. Most student comments on RateMyProfessors.com are very sincere.

66. Use common sense with RateMyProfessors.com.

67. It's almost a good idea to disregard the overall averages and concentrate on the comments.

68. Be like a gold miner and mine the comments for gems of information.

69. There is an abundance of valuable course information in RateMyProfessors.com comments.

70. I researched most of my former professors and found the ratings and comments on RateMyProfessors.com accurate and reflective of my own experience.

71. A good time to use RateMyProfessors.com is when you are registering for courses and know which professors are teaching what.

72. A course that includes a professor's specialty is going to be good.

73. It is one of the delights of life to be in a class taught by a professor who adores the material.

74. If you like a professor, take him/her as often as possible.

75. Meet with your professor early in the semester if you expect the course to be difficult for you.

76. If you disagree with a professor on an emotional issue, be prepared to suffer with anger or boredom, or don't take that professor's course.

77. Depending on how it's used, the term "dead white male" can be racist and derogatory.

78. Some professors think it is cutesy to pepper their lectures with "dead white male" this and "dead white male" that, but here's how I felt when I first heard it in a serious classroom.

79. It is perverse to taint the people you are teaching about because of their skin color as this rhetoric professor had done.

80. The standard for racism should be equally applied across the board.

81. The overwhelming majority of professors teach their material with great love and vigor, and leave politics out of it.

82. If a course is not that important to you, then take the easiest professor.

83. If you screw up on your first test, go see your professor and tell him/her that you are going for an "A" in the course.

84. Choose carefully the professor who will direct an important paper for you, such as for departmental honors.

85. Professors who direct papers know that other professors often read those papers and NO professor wants something to end up in a paper that might make him/her look bad.

86. If you are in a dispute with a professor, don't let him/her grade you.

87. If you feel that you have been discriminated against by a professor, file a complaint.

88. The undergraduate dean's office will usually be genuinely sympathetic to a student's plight, and not automatically on the side of faculty.

89. I want to make it clear that it is always best to avoid a meltdown.

90. A professor should stick by the syllabus

91. Most professors would never arbitrarily change a syllabus, but it *can* happen.

III
Class

92. You must attend EVERY single class.

93. Class is so important that a student can almost pass in college by just going to class.

94. If there is an earthquake, or you are run over by a bus and have to miss a class, make SURE you get good notes from somebody.

95. You MUST show up for class on time.

96. If you have to brave the elements to get to class, you score big points with your professor, even if you are late.

97. Give your professor the benefit of the doubt if he/she is late to class.

98. Observe a respectful and considerate protocol in class.

99. Don't be seduced into just listening to a class lecture and thinking you'll remember it all later. You WON'T.

100. Use pens or pencils for note-taking, whatever you delight in using.

101. A videotape case is the *perfect* size and structure for pencils, pens, erasers, paper clips, a couple packs of Post-it® Notes, highlighter, etc.

102. Always put sharpened pencils in your case with the points up.

103. Post-it Notes or Sticky Notes® or a generic product are important. So is a highlighter.

104. There will be times in class when you need to mark passages in a book and Post-it or similar sticky notes will save you a *ton* of time.

105. Write down every word a professor says, if possible.

106. Tag anything in a textbook or novel or anywhere else that a professor tells you might be on a test.

107. ESPECIALLY note when a professor says that something is the "most important" or "most controversial" or "most" anything.

108. Write in the margins of books and tag the pages with sticky notes.

109. Sometimes a student under severe time pressure can skip assigned reading material if he/she goes to every class. However, there are NOTABLE exceptions.

110. You should NEVER EVER skip any reading or homework in math, sciences and foreign languages – anything for which your knowledge builds as you progress through the semester.

111. The best thing to do is not get behind in math, sciences and foreign languages, and that includes statistics, economics, and any discipline that works with numbers and formulas.

112. There is a tremendous side benefit to math, sciences and foreign languages: They *sharpen* the mind like nothing else can.

113. It is good to truly master the basics in lower level language courses. Put a lot into it.

114. Latin can help you learn the Romance languages: Spanish, Portuguese, French, Italian, Romanian and more than a dozen others.

115. Latin is a valuable language to know.

116. Studying a spoken language is exciting too, and can help you in our global world, especially with business.

117. Send emails to fellow students using the foreign language you are studying.

118. If you're in a literature class and can't read a novel, then get a study guide such as CliffsNotes or SparkNotes or equivalent, if available.

119. If a study guide on a certain novel is not available, find something online.

120. Get the classes you want.

121. When scheduling classes, sometimes it is good to have time in between classes.

122. Consider longer classes that meet only once a week.

123. Give yourself as many ways as possible to get in a course you want or need. Stack the odds in your favor.

124. Pay special attention during Drop/Add Week, especially the beginning of Drop/Add Week.

125. One last resort is a Class Override by the professor.

IV
Grades

126. Take advantage of ALL opportunities to boost your grade by class participation.

127. MAKE yourself answer some short-answer questions in class.

128. Don't wait to answer a question. You'll get nervous. Do it quickly!

129. The better you know your assignment, the more you'll *want* to answer questions.

130. If you are shy, you are not alone. A lot of people are petrified of speaking in front of other people.

131. Most participation grades are in smaller classes and not lecture halls.

132. If you haven't read the assignment, use this trick to get your participation grade.

133. Potential love interests will think you are bold and confident.

134. Do all the things that will give you 10% here and there because they add up.

135. Always do extra credit assignments.

136. Ask your professor for extra credit.

137. Always go for "+"s because they make a huge difference in a Grade Point Average (GPA).

138. Develop a grade STRATEGY based on your situation.

139. Make your study time extremely productive.

140. Drop a course if you need to lighten your work load.

141. You learn SO much more when you make "A"s.

142. Making good grades makes you more competitive and mentally tougher.

143. Make it fun: Compete and bet a friend a beer (or a cola if you are underage) on who scores highest on quizzes and tests.

144. Making "A"s will make you more powerful intellectually than making "B"s; but making "B"s will make you more powerful than making "C"s, all other things being even.

145. The more active you are mentally, the smarter and more powerful you will become overall.

146. The trick is to study what you LOVE, and DO what you love.

147. If you need a certain GPA to maintain a scholarship, then focus on it.

148. If you can't drop a course, then be proactive and deal with the load.

V
Studying Effectively

149. Examine your desk calendar at least once a week.

150. Do not study with the TV on or music playing.

151. One can accomplish more in 15 minutes of quiet than in two hours with the TV blaring or music playing.

152. Plan your study time. Take control of your life.

153. Always opt for absolute control over everything.

154. Always follow assignments EXACTLY as given by a professor.

155. The key to good grades is figuring out how to teach yourself material fast and effectively, beyond the usual memory tricks.

156. Create personal study aids for EVERYTHING!

157. Keep your eyes open for any kind of study guide that will help you.

158. Make copies of all articles in periodicals, as well as anything your professor has placed on reserve in the library.

159. Always read the footnotes or endnotes in a scholarly article or book. Make a copy of endnotes.

160. Don't be cheap about copies.

161. Always buy extra things that will help you.

162. Buy additional books if they will help you in a course, especially a foreign language.

163. There is an unlimited supply of helpful things on the Internet, but be careful.

164. Keep valuable handouts on foreign language grammar in a single file folder and close at hand.

165. Turn a file folder into a pouch for all your handouts by stapling the sides.

166. Make POWERFUL study aids by making a copy of the help sections in the back of some books so you have them at your fingertips.

167. My Latin file folder of grammar handouts and aids was awesome and actually made translating fun.

168. When translating a foreign language passage for homework, create practice sheets that break the passage apart sentence by sentence *(see illustration below)*.

169. ALWAYS do ALL homework in math, sciences, foreign languages, statistics, economics ⁃ any course that uses numbers and formulas or for which knowledge builds as you progress through the semester.

170. You can "Google" anything these days, so do it. It enhances study and research.

171. If you can't think of a term or title, Google what you know.

172. Do outside things to help learn an assignment.

173. When reading plays, go see a performance of said play.

174. Look at DVDs on people you are studying, especially literary people whose works you are studying.

175. When reading a novel, taking notes helps enormously.

176. Always put the novel's page number by *each* of your notes.

177. In your notes, jot down the main things as you encounter them in a novel.

178. Always write your thoughts down as you read. If you don't, you'll lose most of them.

179. A trick to use if crunched for time with a novel.

180. CliffsNotes, SparkNotes and similar study guides are helpful.

181. A movie based on a novel will be somewhat different from the novel, and that's OK.

182. Intense school work sharpens the mind.

183. It's not only the knowledge one gains, but abilities and skills are honed.

VI
Preparing for Tests / Exams

184. Make sure you go to ALL classes as you get closer to test time.

185. The class before a test, a professor will usually go over what will be on the test. This is when sticky notes really help.

186. Go to EVERY test review and study session.

187. A videotaped study session is extremely helpful in some courses, especially sciences and math, in which there are problems to solve.

188. Do Exam Preparation Triage when you run out of study time.

189. Exam Preparation Triage works like *MASH*.

190. You might have a more complicated need.

191. While crunched for time in the middle of Exam Preparation Triage, plan smartly.

192. There will be times when you need to forget about what you don't know, and study what you know.

193. MAKE AN "A" ON EVERY SINGLE TEST, GUARANTEED, with my brilliant Unconventionally-Typeset Printouts *(see illustration below)*.

194. A student who gets behind will find my Unconventionally-Typeset Printouts invaluable.

195. If there is no time to type all your notes, then highlight and tag right in your notebook.

196. Let me reiterate that typing the notes from your notebook is a tremendous way to learn test material easily.

197. For math, sciences and foreign languages, there is no substitute for working tons of problems.

198. Create your own practice tests.

199. You can and should create practice tests for most subjects.

200. Create fill-in-the-blank exercises for any subject because they are EXTREMELY helpful.

201. Fill-in-the-blank exercises are especially valuable with foreign languages *(see illustration below)*.

202. Here's another good example of a practice test, this one using a star chart.

203. When preparing for a test, remember the "MOSTS."

204. Note everything a professor emphasizes in a lecture.

205. Marijuana is illegal in most places, but if you smoke pot, DON'T smoke anywhere near an important test or exam.

206. I KNOW how pot works.

207. Smoking pot when doing research for papers will slow or shut you down. Don't waste your valuable time.

208. Most people can not do research while stoned.

209. Don't study when stoned. It is a WASTE of time.

210. Most "brilliant" ideas one gets when stoned have to be discarded the next day anyway.

211. Your mind will sharpen from using it in school, but smoking pot when studying for a test is STUPID.

212. If you have been smoking pot but have an important test approaching, stop smoking and get some exercise to work it out of your system.

213. Exercising is always a great thing to do.

214. Another huge benefit of exercise is stress reduction.

215. Do exercise a lot, and regularly, but don't overdo it the day before a test or even two days before a test.

216. The goal is to be at your PEAK on test day or game day.

217. Get a good night's sleep before a test.

218. Do not go out for a quick beer with friends the night before a test unless you have IRON discipline.

219. Do not encourage friends who have tests the next day to go out with you.

220. If you fail a test, and your final exam is cumulative, make SURE you get all the correct answers so you won't miss them on the final.

221. You might be able to pull up a failed test, so earn as many points as you can.

VII
Taking Tests / Exams

222. Professors hate sloppy tests. Be neat with everything.

223. Consider erasable ink for exams.

224. When you are handed your exam and your professor says you can look at it, glance at the *whole* thing, so you know what you are dealing with, then quickly answer all the questions you know.

225. Make SURE you don't miss any pages or extra credit questions.

226. Make SURE you allot your time correctly.

227. Even within sections of an exam, you must be allot your time correctly.

228. Start with the essay question you can answer best and fastest, then go to the one you can answer next best and fastest, then finally the one you have to wrestle with.

229. Just DON'T get hung-up on a question.

230. Outline discussion answers in the margin, and be neat.

231. Always write things down as they occur to you.

232. Jot notes in the margin on anything that might help answer a question, but stay neat.

233. If you run out of time, make SURE you at least outline all the essay questions. The outline can get you some credit.

234. Often the answer to a skipped question can be found in another question later in the test.

235. It is best to go with your first answer to a question.

236. Hold the bull manure to a minimum.

237. Sometime take-home exams can work you harder than a regular in-class exam.

VIII
Papers and Writing

238. Anything you have to research and write, you are going to learn well.

239. Make sure you understand from your professor the exact way he/she wants your paper written and cited.

240. Forget "easy." Choose topics that you are dying to learn about. You'll be motivated and enjoy it more.

241. Consider topics that will help you in other parts of a course, or in a different course.

242. Decide on paper topics as QUICKLY as possible.

243. Once you choose your topic, spend a little time with it as soon as you can and develop at least a tentative research strategy.

244. Make SURE the books you need for research are available.

245. Papers can sneak up on you.

246. The worst thing to do is wait until the last minute to start a paper.

247. For many history, political science and literature courses, a general history fact finder is an invaluable aid.

248. A desk encyclopedia is also valuable.

249. CliffsNotes, SparkNotes or their equivalent can aid in your research, especially if it is literary.

250. Don't hesitate to Google anything! . . . especially while you are sitting at your desk researching and writing.

251. Wikipedia will usually pop up first or close to first, and it is usually extremely helpful.

252. If you are not sure of a spelling, type in what you know and if it is incorrect, usually Google will suggest the correct spelling.

253. You can use a thesaurus to find a correct spelling if you are not at your computer.

254. Read primary sources as often as possible when writing history papers.

255. Secondary sources are interpretations of history by later scholars.

256. Be aware of the scourge of political correctness on scholarship and free speech.

257. You can not possibly understand history by using today's standards to judge the past.

258. Political correctness is ignorance and leads to a total lack of historical understanding.

259. Southern history as it is taught today is a "cultural and political atrocity," and students are being CHEATED.

260. Young students of history and literature should examine everything.

261. Those historians with a vested interest in maintaining that slavery caused the war, are not telling you the truth. They are cheating you out of understanding much of American history.

262. Another major issue was unfair taxation - British taxes were a huge issue in 1776 but were minuscule compared to what the South was paying in 1861.

263. Be a scholar.

264. Write what you want.

265. Research for papers is why you need to be on great terms with EVERYBODY in the library.

266. When researching, it is often good to start with an encyclopedia article as an overview.

267. Examine the bibliography or works cited section in articles and books in which you are doing research because they will suggest other sources.

268. Look for additional sources of information on people and topics you are studying.

269. Of course, NEVER have the TV on or music playing when writing.

270. Do what a lot of writers do to improve their writing: Read what other writers say about writing.

271. There is a rhythm and balance to good prose.

272. The best writing is easy to read.

273. Newspaper-style writing is powerful and effective. Here's good advice from Ernest Hemingway and Professor Strunk.

274. Reread (or read) E. B. White's essay on writing in *The Elements of Style*: "An Approach to Style (With a List of Reminders)."

275. Ask your professor if he/she has an example of an "A" paper like the one you are required to write. Do this for any paper you have to write in any course.

276. If you know what you want to say, and you have done good research, your paper will burst out of you.

277. Once you start writing, stay focused like a laser.

278. Write your first draft in a white heat . . . or not.

279. Develop your own style of writing. Do what works for you.

280. You must put most of the clay on the potter's wheel before you can shape it.

281. If you get stuck, you must quickly get UNstuck.

282. I almost had a disaster in English 650 because I got stuck.

283. It did drop my "A" in the course down to a "B+", but it taught me two VALUABLE lessons.

284. Sleep on any kind of writing, ALWAYS.

285. Never do final editing on anything that is hand-written, if you can help it.

286. It's a good idea to do final editing from printed pages and not the computer screen, if you have time.

287. For a book review, read the book thoroughly, take notes, underline, highlight and tag pages as you read.

288. You might want to read what others have said about the book. Or not.

289. Always cite your sources and record bibliographical information as you go along.

290. Popular styles of citation are MLA, APA, Chicago Style and Turabian Style, though there are numerous others depending on the field.

291. The information needed for a bibliographical or works cited entry is contained in footnotes/endnotes, and vice versa. Here's a Chicago Style example.

292. If your word processor won't help with the bibliography, simply paste the citation information at the end of your paper as you write.

293. Save your paper's word processing file REGULARLY as you work! The keystrokes are simple and fast.

294. Always create TWO files of anything you are working on in case you accidentally delete the main one, or the main one becomes corrupted. Here's an easy way to do it. *(This is a repeat from Chapter 1, but worth repeating here).*

295. Save individual files you are working on to both your master folder AND the master folder backup on your flash drive. *(This is a repeat from Chapter 1, but worth repeating here).*

296. Also back up your work to a CD or DVD, something that is separate from your computer in case your computer blows up. *(This is a repeat from Chapter 1, but worth repeating here).*

297. Consider subscribing to a service that backs up your files automatically. *(This is a repeat from Chapter 1, but worth repeating here).*

298. BE EXTREMELY CAREFUL when copying files and folders. You can destroy all your work if you aren't. *(This is a repeat from Chapter 1, but worth repeating here).*

299. A deleted file will stay in your Recycle Bin until you use the "Empty the Recycle Bin" command. *(This is a repeat from Chapter 1, but worth repeating here).*

300. It's worth repeating: NEVER, EVER turn in an essay you picked up on the Internet as your own.

IX
Presentations

301. If you can walk and read, you can do a presentation.

302. If you have a choice, do a presentation on a topic that really interests you!

303. Make sure you follow your professor's instructions to the letter. Always do this with any assignment.

304. Make the print much larger in the document or notes from which you will be presenting.

305. The days before your presentation, read out loud.

306. Speak with a strong voice. Don't be a shrinking violet or wimp.

307. Videotape yourself at home, or record your voice as you practice.

308. Practice making eye contact with the class.

309. Put your finger on your place in your notes as you look up at the class.

310. Visualize yourself walking confidently up to the podium and giving a great presentation.

311. Visualization works for all human endeavors.

312. On presentation day, wear clothes that make you confident, drink a little water to loosen vocal cords and go to the bathroom.

313. Walk up to the podium with confidence. "Physicalize" the way actors do.

314. During your presentation, DO NOT EVER say you are nervous.

315. I watched a fellow give a good presentation in a class then ruin it by saying that he knew he was "boring" and couldn't continue.

316. Use transparencies or other visual aids to help with nervousness and to help cue you. Your talk will be more interesting.

317. Use of visual aids will impress your professor.

318. If you can, go into your classroom before class and practice.

319. Make sure your notes and visual aids are in order.

320. Do a PowerPoint® presentation.

321. Don't chicken-out of doing a presentation. If you do, you will likely be penalized.

322. If you are also nervous about asking or answering questions in class MAKE yourself get over that too.

X
Continue Strong
Winning, and the Philosophy of Success

323. Read about success and those who have achieved it.

324. Accumulate a library of success books and refer back to them regularly.

325. Buy the old classic, *Think and Grow Rich*, by Napoleon Hill.

326. Buy *The Power of Positive Thinking*, by Norman Vincent Peale.

327. Another classic is the huge 1936 bestseller, *How to Win Friends and Influence People*, by Dale Carnegie.

328. *The Art of War*, by Sun Tzu, edited by James Clavell, is an enlightening book of strategy and success.

329. Planning is also essential in life!

330. Read the autobiography of Wal-Mart founder, Sam Walton.

331. Read some of Donald Trump's books.

332. When you read an exceptionally motivational quotation, look up the person saying it and read a brief bio. Learn something about an accomplished person.

333. Compilations of success quotations are jam-packed with crackling, buzzing electricity.

334. The most powerful success material I ever read was compiled by an American philosopher and writer, Elbert Hubbard, and published in 1923 with title *Elbert Hubbard's Scrap Book.*

335. *Elbert Hubbard's Scrap Book* is powerful.

336. Here are a few of the most powerful quotations for me from *Elbert Hubbard's Scrap Book.*

337. Other quotations by Elbert Hubbard himself.

338. Find and clip stirring words anywhere, and make them yours.

339. There are excellent success-quotation websites on the Internet. Search for "success quotations."

340. Another good website is www.BrainyQuote.com. Here are a few from H. L. Mencken

341. More from www.BrainyQuote.com:

342. Know Vince Lombardi, immortal coach of the Green Bay Packers, who won the first two Super Bowls and never had a losing record in the NFL.

343. Other quotations by Vince Lombardi.

344. Powerful statements about Vince Lombardi by some of his players, from the book *Lombardi, Winning Is the Only Thing*, edited by Jerry Kramer.

345. If you draw power from other sources such as your faith or family, then nurture them too. Nurture all sources of power.

346. Do things that give you confidence. I ran four marathons!

347. I was determined to graduate magna cum laude, one of the greatest goals of my life.

348. And now my goal is to show YOU how to do it!

349. Do things that discourage self-consciousness.

350. Keep your body strong and fit.

351. America is a land of unlimited opportunity.

Author's Final Note

If you graduated from college with honors,
please be in the next edition of this book with a
testimonial telling how you did it! I want to know
about your raw determination and drive, sleepless
nights researching, writing, studying, fights with
professors, **innovative techniques** and your final
victory of walking across the stage as your name
is called with the words cum laude, magna cum
laude, or summa cum laude, behind it.

My goal is to INSPIRE other people and help
them achieve academic success too! I'm looking for
1,000 words or so by people who graduated with
honors from any accredited college or university
on the planet.

I can not pay you, but your contribution will help
others and will give you and your school some
well-deserved recognition in an excellent book.

Not everyone will be selected, but I want to
THANK EVERYONE who writes to me! My email
address is GK@CharlestonAthenaeumPress.com.

If you find a typo in this book, please email me.

I am NOT receiving a kickback, commission or
any compensation whatsoever of any kind from

ANY product, service or place mentioned in this book such as Post-it notes, Sticky Notes, CliffsNotes, SparkNotes, Monarch Notes, Kim Komando, Carbonite, RateMyProfessors.com, the College of Charleston, The Citadel, Encyclopedia Britannica Online, Atlantis Word Processor, Longman, Pearson, any entity associated with *The Elements of Style*, Donald Trump, Wal-Mart, QuotationsPage.com, BrainyQuote.com or any other entity.

The names of common products mentioned in this book are trademarks of the companies owning them, and some of them are generic names as well, e.g., Sticky Notes® and sticky notes.

A few things in this book are repeated, here and there, because they fit well in more than one chapter.

Additional information is on our websites, www.CharlestonAthenaeumPress.com and www.ElementsOfAcademicSuccess.com.

Many many heartfelt thanks to the talented young lady who designed the new book cover under the direction of the author. This gorgeous design was created by Sanja Stojilkovic. She can be reached by email at ichnjisan@yahoo.com.

I can not guarantee that a person reading this book will graduate magna cum laude from college BUT I CAN GUARANTEE that these techniques are outstanding and highly effective and absolutely worked for the author. They are PROVEN beyond the shadow of a doubt, and they can certainly work for you!

Colophon

This book is typeset like Strunk and White's legendary book, *The Elements of Style,* with numbered, easy-to-read, bold topic sentences introducing each topic section.

The book is designed for ease of use and speed for busy students to go through with maximum comprehension. That's why left aligned (ragged right) text was chosen, rather than justified text. Studies show that ragged right text with its uniform spacing between words is easier to read and comprehend.

This is a 6 x 9 inch book with 1 inch top, bottom and outside margins, and 1.1 inches inside.

There are a total of 351 numbered bold topic sentences in 10 chapters, and each bold topic sentence is Century 12 point bold, single spaced, with first line indented .3 inches.

Body text is Century 12 point with 1.1 line spacing and first lines indented .3 inches.

The "Author's Note" and similar section titles are Century 14 point bold.

Chapter titles are Century 16 point bold, and

Chapters I and X include subtitles that are Century 16 point italic.

Chapter epigraphs are Century 12 point italic indented .3 inches left and right, with no first line indent.

All type in the "Index of All 351 Bold Topic Sections by Chapter" is Century 11 point, single spaced, with first lines indented .3 inches.

There are seven illustrations.

The five study guides are actual study guides created by the author and used in his classes at the College of Charleston.

The captions are 10 point bold Verdana with 1.2 line spacing.

The text inside the headers at the top of each page including page numbers, as well as any page numbers in footers at the bottom of pages, are Century 11 point.

Small Roman numerals were used for all the front material, and Arabic numerals used in the rest of the book.

This book was typeset using Atlantis Word Processor, Version 1.6.5.11. A slightly earlier version of Atlantis was used to typeset the eBook.

Study guides were graphically improved using ancient Photoshop 5.5.

All writing, editing and typesetting for the eBook and print version of *The Elements of Academic Success* were done by the author.

Bibliography

American Psychological Association. Citation information on Wikipedia. Accessed March 27, 2013. http://en.wikipedia.org/wiki/APA_style.

Beowulf, CliffsNotes. Stanley P. Baldwin, Author. Foster City, CA: IDG Books Worldwide, Inc., 2000.

BrainyQuote. Quotations website. Accessed March 28, 2013. http://www.BrainyQuote.com.

Carbonite. Automatic online file backup service. Accessed March 25, 2013. http://www.Carbonite.com

Carnegie, Dale. *How to Win Friends and Influence People.* Reprint, New York: Simon & Schuster, 2009. First published 1936.

Chicago Manual of Style, The. Citation information on their website. Accessed March 27, 2013. http://www.chicagomanualofstyle.org/tools_citationguide.html.

Evans, Walker. Exhibit of his photography including photographs and memorabilia of Ernest Hemingway, and photographs of Charleston, South Carolina. Gibbes Museum of Art, Charleston, SC, February 2, 2006.

Farrell, Susan Elizabeth. *Critical Companion to Kurt Vonnegut.* New York: Facts on File, 2008; *Critical Companion to Tim O'Brien.* New York: Facts on File, 2011. Both are from the Facts on File Library of American Literature.

Farrow, Anne, Joel Lang, and Jenifer Frank. *Complicity, How the North Promoted, Prolonged, and Profited from Slavery.* New York: Ballantine Books, 2005.

Fisher, Jim. Columnist of *The Kansas City Star.* "Ernest Hemingway and *The Kansas City Star* / Of '*Star* Style' and a reporter named Hemingway." *The Kansas City Star* website. Accessed March 26, 2013. http://www.kcstar.com/hemingway/hem3.shtml.

Gallup. "Conservatives Remain the Largest Ideological Group in U.S." Article on Gallup website by Lydia Saad dated January 12, 2012 based on a Gallup Poll. Accessed March 25, 2013. http://www.gallup.com/poll/152021/conservatives-remain-largest-ideological-group.aspx.

Genovese, Eugene D. *The Southern Tradition, The Achievement and Limitations of an American Conservatism*. Cambridge, MA and London: Harvard University Press, 1994.

Hill, Napoleon. *Think and Grow Rich*. Reprinted as *Think and Grow Rich: The Landmark Bestseller-Now Revised and Updated for the 21st Century*. Revised and expanded by Arthur R. Pell. New York: Jeremy P. Tarcher/Penguin, 2005. First published 1937.

Hubbard, Elbert. *Elbert Hubbard's Scrap Book*. New York: Wm. H. Wise & Co., Roycroft Distributors, 1923.

Hugo, Victor. Quotation in *Elbert Hubbard's Scrap Book*. New York: Wm. H. Wise & Co., Roycroft Distributors, 1923.

King, Stephen. *On Writing, A Memoir of the Craft*. New York: Pocket Books, 2000.

Kizer, Jr., Gene H. "Economic Arguments and Justifications for Southern Secession, 1850s to 1861." Bachelor's Essay, College of Charleston, 2000, Addlestone Library Special Collections.

Kramer, Jerry, ed. *Winning Is the Only Thing*. New York: The World Publishing Company, 1970.

Lombardi, Vince. "What It Takes to be Number One" on Vince Lombardi website. Accessed March 28, 2013. http://www.vincelombardi.com/number-one.html.

Merriam-Webster's Collegiate Encyclopedia. Springfield, MA: Merriam-Webster, Inc. and Encyclopedia Britannica, Inc., 2000.

Microsoft. Information on files and folders. Accessed March 25, 2013. http://www.Windows.Microsoft.com, then search for "files and folders."

Modern Language Association. Citation information on website. Accessed March 27, 2013. http://www.MLA.org/style.

Peale, Norman Vincent. *The Power of Positive Thinking.* Reprint, New York: Ishi Press International, 2011. First published 1952.

Perkins, Howard Cecil, ed. *Northern Editorials on Secession*, Volumes I and II. Reprint, Gloucester, MA: Peter Smith, 1964. First published 1942 by The American Historical Association and Appleton-Century-Crofts, Inc.

Quotations Page, The. Quotations website. Accessed March 28, 2013. http://www.quotationspage.com.

RateMyProfessors. Website for evaluating college professors. Accessed March 25, 2013. http://www.RateMyProfessors.com.

Strunk, Jr., William, and E. B. White. *The Elements of Style*. Fourth Edition. New York: Longman, 2000.

Trump, Donald J., and Bill Zanker. *Think Big and Kick Ass, in Business and Life*. New York: HarperCollins, 2007.

Turabian Style. Citation information on Wikipedia. Accessed March 27, 2013. en.wikipedia.org/wiki/A_Manual_for_Writers_ of_Research_Papers,_Theses,_and_ Dissertations.

Tzu, Sun. *The Art of War*. Edited by James Clavell. New York: Delacorte Press, 1983.

United Technologies. Ad entitled "To the Kid on the End of the Bench." *Wall Street Journal*, December 5, 1985.

Walton, Sam, with John Huey. *Made in America, My Story*. New York: Doubleday, 1992.

White, E. B. "An Approach to Style (With a List of Reminders)." In William Strunk, Jr. and E. B. White *The Elements of Style*. Fourth Edition. New York: Longman, 2000.

Wikimedia Commons. Accessed March 26, 2013.
    http://commons.wikimedia.org/wiki/
    Main_Page.

Yanak, Ted, and Pam Cornelison. *The Great
    American History Fact Finder.* Boston:
    Houghton Mifflin Company, 1993.

Zinsser, William. *On Writing Well, The Classic
    Guide to Writing Nonfiction.* 30th
    Anniversary Edition, Seventh Edition. New
    York: Collins, 2006.

Finis

Charleston Athenaeum Press